W9-CKD-329

TOWARD A
CIVIL SOCIETY

TOWARD A CIVIL SOCIETY

Civic Literacy
and Service Learning

C. DAVID LISMAN

BERGIN & GARVEY
Westport, Connecticut • London

Library of Congress Cataloging-in-Publication Data

Lisman, C. David.
 Toward a civil society : civic literacy and service learning / C.
David Lisman.
   p. cm.
 Includes bibliographical references (p.   ) and index.
 ISBN 0–89789–566–5 (alk. paper).—ISBN 0–89789–567–3 (pbk. :
alk. paper)
  1. Student service—United States. 2. Education, Higher—Social
aspects—United States. 3. Civics—Study and teaching (Higher)—
United States. I. Title.
 LC220.5.L57 1998
 306.43′2—dc21   98–11067

British Library Cataloguing in Publication Data is available.

Library of Congress Catalog Card Number: 98–11067
ISBN: 0–89789–566–5
   . 0–89789–567–3 (pbk.)

First published in 1998

Bergin & Garvey, 88 Post Road West, Westport, CT 06881
An imprint of Greenwood Publishing Group, Inc.

Printed in the United States of America

The paper used in this book complies with the
Permanent Paper Standard issued by the National
Information Standards Organization (Z39.48–1984).

10 9 8 7 6 5 4 3 2 1

For my wife, a life-long educator, my colleagues in service learning, and those we serve

Contents

1. The Need for a Civil Society   1

2. The Concept of the Civil Society and Weak and Strong Democracy   13

3. Service Learning   23

4. Service Learning as Volunteerism and the Neoconservative Theory of Civic Literacy   45

5. Service Learning as Experiential Education and Consumerist Politics   59

6. Service Learning as Justice   75

7. Service Learning and Strong Democracy   89

8. A Community-Development Approach to Service Learning   117

9. Principles and Best Practices of Campus and Community Partnerships   127

10. The Social Responsibilities of Higher Education   149

Works Cited   163

Index   173

TOWARD A
CIVIL SOCIETY

1

The Need for a Civil Society

We need to become a more civil society, for we are suffering from a civic malaise. Two stories from the Netherlands illustrate what we are facing. We are familiar with the story of the Dutch boy who saved his town from a flood by putting his finger in the dike. This story contrasts with one from Holland aired a couple of years ago on National Public Radio in which a man claimed he found a set of false teeth inside a fish and returned then to its owner. However, it turned out the fisherman had played a trick. He had put a set of his wife's teeth inside the fish. The person who got the dentures finally admitted that they had never really fit very well.

These two stories provide contrasting images. The first illustrates heroic commitment to community. The second highlights our concern that many people lack a sense of social commitment. In this case, lack of social commitment took the form of someone playing a deceptive trick on someone else and taking advantage of a general sense of social trust. We would like to believe that people's words and deeds are not deceptive. But we all have become more cautious in our dealings with people.

One can expect a lack of social commitment in times of social stress involving a sense of ethical fracturing in the civic infrastructure. Respective groups become competitive rather than cooperative whenever it appears to one group that another group is not pulling its own weight. Thus, social dis-functionality undermines our commitment to society. In the best of times a lack of societal commitment can be problematic. But in times of great social stress, a society without the civic resources to collaborate in solving its problems is in great danger of further fragmentation. We are seeing symptoms of such divisiveness.

We are facing a variety of complex social issues and angry responses. Crime and gang activities proliferate with many advocating a policy of getting tough on crime without a willingness to address its root causes. The gap between the wealthy and the poor widens, as an increasingly disgruntled and conservative middle class blames the government and the poor for its problems and becomes increasingly apathetic to seeking public solutions for its concerns. Consequently, conservative legislators have passed a welfare reform bill that eliminates the safety net for the poorest among us; they also call for further government cutbacks in spending and a reduction in taxes, while ignoring the fact that the great disparity of wealth between the rich and the poor is a significant source of the problem of poverty.

We also are experiencing a weakening of the institution of the family as evidenced by the reporting of increased child abuse and neglect, a high divorce rate, and fathers avoiding child support payments. A contentious African-American splinter group, which was epitomized by the Million Man March—a gathering of African-American males in Washington, DC to promote greater family responsibility—fans the flames of multicultural divisiveness. The so-called patriot movement can be understood as partly the product of increasing social alienation in which the civic process is seen as the "enemy" rather than as a resource. Wealthy conservatives have succeeded in pitting the middle class against the poor, thereby diverting attention from the role of corporate power in the contribution of declining wages and a consequential undermining of civil life in our local communities.

A corporate climate is developing that does not value loyalty as it did in the past, casting out many angry and bewildered workers in the interest of greater profits for stakeholders. Workforce needs are changing in our increasingly advanced technological society, leaving many people underemployed and unsure of how to cope with this changing workforce environment. Increased computerized automation in the work place has produced just-in-time employment and downsizing (Rifkin, 1995). Wages for blue- and white-collar workers have declined or remained stagnant while corporate wealth has increased. A recent report indicates that corporate executives have received an average wage increase of over 50% during this past year as compared to an average of a 3% raise for the working class. Linked to these changing workforce patterns, our society is experiencing a loss of manufacturing to the global market, which often involves exploitation of Third World workers. Worldwide, we are experiencing environmental degradation through the depletion of the ozone layer, the threat of the greenhouse effect, and the dwindling of natural resources such as water.

Developing social policies to cope effectively with these problems and issues requires a citizenry possessing a broad understanding of the interdependence of people, social institutions, and communities and an enhanced ability both to draw upon and further develop this knowledge as they confront human problems (Stanton, 1990, p. 178). We especially need to attain a deeper understanding of the difference between intermediate problems, such as drug use and crime, from root causes, such as poverty. We also need to develop strategies for addressing our problems locally. However, as we face this need, we have a citizenry isolated from one another and civically disconnected, who all too often turn to privatized solutions to our social problems.

An example of this privatization is the conservative movement to reestablish family values, in which this endeavor is attempted in isolation while neglecting the negative environmental factors that weaken the family. The 1995 Republican presidential candidate Bob Dole succinctly expressed this conservative outlook when he said that it does not take a village to raise a child, but a family. So instead of being engaged in strategic planning on workforce development to help low-income families gain new job skills, people offer parenting classes or suggest books of stories that can promote moral development of the individual.

The growing alienation from government itself is another example of our civic breakdown, which I have already referred to in the context of the "patriot movement." The failed effort of Newt Gingrich and his fellow Republicans to pass the "New Contract for America" legislation, jokingly referred to as the "Contract on America," typifies our civic isolationism. This breached effort reveals an anti-government attitude in wanting severely to limit government, reduce taxation, and provide term limitations. A report a couple of years ago indicating that college freshman are more apolitical than ever and disinterested in debating politics is another example of civic disenfranchisement. More recently, according to UCLA's annual survey of college freshmen, these students are feeling less connected with academics and politics than any entering class in the 32-year history of the survey (CIRP Press Release, 1997).

What is the cause of our civic disconnection? Does it reside, as some think, in political gridlock? Or is it the fault of the citizenry? Barber (1992) and Etzioni (1993) both claim that there is an "uncoupling of rights and responsibilities." It is alleged that too many people are demanding or expecting something from their government without being willing to accept the responsibility to help support the civic infrastructure upon which they are making demands. But there is more to it than this. Elshtain, in a recent essay (1997), restates in slightly different wording her point from her earlier book (1995). She says that we are experiencing a "spiral of delegitimization" partly caused by a new form of plebiscitary democracy "that reduces voters and legislators alike to passive (albeit angry) consumers and instruments (1997, p. 11). Government has taken on an increasing number of "wedge issues," such as abortion, family values, and race relations "that treat 'blacks' and 'whites' as though they were homogeneous interest groups, rather than collectives themselves divided by regional, religious, class, and other lines" (1997, p. 11).

People have not just made a conscious decision to give up on politics in a way they might have had grown tired of a hobby. Our civic disaffection is entangled with all too human and political/economic factors that have undermined our commitment to upholding the common good. Individuals have become increasingly isolated from one another, maximizing their own self-interest at the expense of others.

To use a phrase from Habermas, we are experiencing a legitimation crises (Taylor, 1994). A society has legitimacy when its members so understand and value society that they are willing to assume the disciplines and burdens that membership entails (Taylor, 1994). Taylor describes this problem as being due to hypertrophy. This literally means the excessive development of an organ. In North America, claims Taylor, we suffer from an excess of independence. We face the risk of societal destruction through an excess of our essential qualities. While we are experiencing an excess of independence, we are witnessing an atrophy of our commitment to the common good.

That the breakdown of our civic infrastructure is attributable to the political/economic form of our hypertrophy is one of the central theses of this book. It would be too simplistic to blame the market economy as the sole culprit, but surely this is part of the problem. However, the corporate capitalistic role in this process can not be completely untangled from our own hubris, our tendency to self-aggrandizement, and to the history of our own country that has placed freedom and political independence as the highest priority when we broke away from Europe and formed a republican form of government. All of these forces have become enmeshed.

As an example of our hypertrophy, we find ourselves supporting our consumer economy, even though we may be cynical about it. The efficacious industrial consumer society "delivers the goods." This consumer attitude reinforces our instrumental stance toward nature that is meant to be a spiritual declaration of independence from it (Taylor, 1994, p. 64). Many believe that our dignity consists in our capacity to dominate, and not to be dominated by, things. Taylor (1994) observes: "If more people are willing to accept a 'permissive' society today, it is because they see that such self-indulgence can be combined with the free self-direction whereby we determine our own purpose and fulfillment" (p. 64). Should they be seen as degenerating into mere self-indulgence, then the society undergoes a crises of confidence. Taylor adds that "our pursuit of efficacy as producers has come to threaten our efficacy as citizens. Freedom as mobility has begun to destroy the very conditions, in family and citizen's community, of freedom itself" (Taylor, p. 70).

Characteristics of our hypertrophy is found in work itself. For many work is "dull, monotonous, without meaning, soul-destroying. We accept alienated labor in return for consumer affluence" (Taylor, p. 65). Taylor further observes: "The development of the affluent society, in which the majority can preside over a self-contained life in adequate private space, has thus gone along with a tacit reluctance to challenge the regime of alienated, subordinate labor" (p. 65). We experience a lack of control over priorities both individually and collectively. The corporate capitalist machine must be allowed to run on. Our collective silence on priorities seems to constitute the condition of our freedom to build our own private spaces and live our own self-contained lives. We fetishize commodities as we become increasingly materialistic, which is another aspect of our hypertrophy is that. This condition is reinforced through the commodification of work and popular culture. Marx (1964) worried that virtual enslavement of workers to the capitalist machine in which workers sell their labor power for mere survival would produce alienation. Certainly this does not represent the current profile of blue- or white-collar workers. Nevertheless, alienating forces are present in the workplace. Rifkin (1995) and others have pointed out that as a result of increased technology leading to downsizing, many workers find themselves underemployed and performing routinized tasks in contrast to the more intellectual work they may have been doing formerly as middle managers. Others have found their work to consist of mainly observing computers and coordinating robotic tasks that originally were performed by assembly line workers. Still others are finding themselves having to work harder and longer hours, never really able to get away from their work because of cellular phones, the fax, the Internet, voice- and e-mail. Increasingly advertisers list their Web site, suggesting that to really keep informed as to the latest developments of just about everything, we should keep busy on the Web! Many of us are beginning to feel as if we are mere technological appendages. Commodification of work is alive, if not well.

The commodification of our work causes us to tend to interpret our lives in a commodified way, which is one of the implications of Marxist theory.

This ironically feeds into advertising and commercialization that encourage us to become materialist consumers. Television commercials and other forms of advertisements entice us with an unending array of goods and services, leaving us with the feeling that we can never acquire enough. The very success of the growth of consumption tends to discredit the importance attached to material gains: the more we have, the less we enjoy what we have. The dominant values of our society, reinforced by the nature of work and by commercialization, reinforce civic disengagement. This constitutes one of the challenges we face in attempting to promote a greater sense of civic engagement in addressing our social and economic concerns.

Our tendency to replace normative issues concerning social purposes with technocratic proposals is another aspect of this phenomenon. According to Habermas (1974), it is difficult from this vantage point to distinguish between practical and technical power. This has resulted in the reduction of theory or rationality to a process of seeking sociotechnical control rather than in an attempt to obtain an existentially and socially meaningful understanding of the purposes of human life. A tendency exists to dismiss humanities-informed approaches that discuss the importance of interrogating the worthwhileness of life and basing decisions on what serves the common good (Taylor, 1989)

Another way of saying this is that we have a tendency to replace more subtle and complicated forms of moral and social investigation with instrumental reason (Taylor, 1991). Instrumental reason is rampant in our approach to understanding our society. For example, this perspective occurs in discussions of the economy. Economists discuss cycles of inflation and recession, creating the impression that our society and others are held captive to a kind of economic determinism that we can do little about. This kind of discussion supplants or minimizes discussions about whether the economy should be structured in the way it is and whether social and political efforts should be mounted through the democratic process to improve society. Not only is this technocratic outlook seriously questionable, but it tends to discourage efforts to challenge the existing economic hegemony. It fuels a sense of fatalism and undermines efforts at economic transformation aimed at reducing the growing gap between the haves and have-nots in our society.

Instrumental reason also creates a momentum of providing national priorities that are amenable to scientific and technocratic manipulation. Hence, much effort is spent on addressing health problems, improving farming techniques, and developing ever more sophisticated objects of consumption. But most of us realize that improved farming techniques or even medical advances can only take us so far. We must consider the question of how we deal with economic inequality, urban sprawl, misuse of our land and water resources, limited medical resources and especially its limited availability to impoverished families and individuals, and with the negative effects of excessive materialism. These problems are not solvable through technological advances alone; they require much social debate and prioritizing through the democratic processes concerning our vision of the good life and the good society and ways that we may realize this vision. Surely technology can be a great asset to the achievement of our vision. But it can not replace our vision.

Unfortunately, technocratic dominance tends to undermine the attempt civically to reclaim our social priorities. We are inclined to seek the opinion of experts as we engage in civic deliberation. Too often these very experts frame the problems in self-serving ways that are not amenable to civic solutions. Our civic efforts are often impeded by accompanying social and political perspectives that promote an ethos of individualism and a non-systemic understanding of social and economic forces. Our scientific and technological biases overpower normative forms of individual and social understanding.

The prevalent sense of our self as "privatized selves" is another manifestation of our hypertrophy. This is manifested through the ideology of individualism in which the individual is seen as the sole reality (Bellah et al., 1985). The plethora of self-help books and television programs has emphasized the goal of self-fulfillment, whether it be discovering our inner child, coping with individual stress, or finding some other source of inner inspiration for overcoming our problems.

Seen from the perspective of the dialectic between our higher sense of purpose and our fears that we may be victimized by rational and technological forces, seeking a deeper sense of self is certainly worthy and understandable—whether it be through seeking inner serenity through Eastern religions or through reading books such as Thomas Moore's *Care of the Soul* (1992). But a kind of frenzy of self-preoccupation persists as an avoidance of confronting the underlying social sources of our malaise or anomie. Talk shows publicize our innermost private feelings and actions. I saw an advertisement on one talk show asking viewers to contact the show if they are white females who have an overweight sister dating their black boyfriend! Anna Freud points out that as parents have adopted a permissive approach to parenting, in reducing the superego or internalization of social authority, they have produced the deepest of all anxieties, that is, the fear of human beings who feel unprotected against the pressure of their drives. With no social restraints, we come to find our own lives empty and fear our own impulses.

Our privatized approach, reinforced by corporate capitalistic forces, tends to encourage us to frame social problems in privatized terms, for instance, blaming the poor for poverty, relying on charity as a way to mitigate the plight of the homeless and economically disadvantaged, and advocating vouchers for schools. This overemphasis on privatization aggravates our social problems, many of which I have already mentioned. These include the fragmentation of the family resulting from a lack of commitment to something besides one's own self. For example, a high percentage of spouses say they have had affairs, and a high divorce rate exists. The case could even be made that elitism in government is linked to our privatism. We leave government to professionals, while setting them up for failure. The failure of President Bill Clinton's attempt during his first term of office to restructure the health care system can be seen as being due to a certain arrogance in the belief that he could "impose" or "sell" America on needed reforms that must come through grass-roots politics.

Moral disengagement is another example of our privatism is. This is seen in the growth of moral subjectivism, the view that moral values are merely a matter of opinion, and relativism, the belief that each person's opinion is as right as anyone else's (Pratte, 1988). Activities such as ethics education are worthy as partial remedies. However, no single approach can cope with the systemic problems we are facing. Unless the community and educational institutions work together to address such problems systemically, these isolated efforts will doubtless be ineffective.

It is in this context of civic crises that many are calling for a need of renewal of civic purpose. We must become a more civil society. Many publications of late, including Barber (1984, 1992), Boyte (1989), Evans and Boyte (1986), McKenzie (1994), and Matthews (1994) advocate the importance of developing a more participatory form of democracy as a way to promote a more civil society. I hope this book can make a positive contribution to this clarion call. I hope to accomplish two goals with this work. One is to help clarify how the service-learning movement can be an effective pedagogy for enlisting the support and activities of our institutions of higher education in contributing to the refurbishment of our civic infrastructure and promoting a more civil society. In the following chapters, I attempt to explain how this movement can be an effective force for civic development. I explain some of the basic aspects of service learning for those who may not be familiar with this movement. At the same time, I discuss ways that educational innovation can be more effective than it currently is in promoting civic literacy.

The second purpose of this book is to draw upon critical pedagogy and liberal communitarian theory to deepen the analysis of civic literacy. Writers such as Barber, Boyte, and Matthews, as much as I admire their work, place too much faith in the "power" of people to come together as a public and work on community issues and concerns. Unfortunately, the lens through which we view society—and thereby view each other in community—is infected by the virus of privatism and by the hegemonic values of corporate America. It also is affected by our hypertrophy. Effective civic efforts must include appropriate analyses of the context in which civic decisions will be made. Above all, with respect to every urgent social concern, whether it be drugs, crime, unemployment, racism, or family breakdown, it is important that these problems be understood in terms of their root causes; and it is also important to point out ways in which hegemony and our ideology of privatism encourage us to not seek to understand the root causes.

An empowered public, working effectively at the local level through local associations and mediating institutions, armed with a sense of civic purpose and tools of social and political analysis, can be a potent force for social and economic change in our country. Moreover, the service learning movement can help link the resources of higher education to the community as a partner in this great civic effort, while at the same time contributing to the development of students who have greater civic and critical capacities. Tendencies of privatism, as exemplified by the charity approach, have infected the service learning movement itself. This endeavor favors having students perform direct service to social agencies with no regard to developing educational and community strategies for reducing or eliminating the problems that give rise to the need for social service agencies such as homeless shelters, shelters for abused women, and youth mentoring programs. The provision of direct social services is not wrong; it is just insufficient as an approach to service learning.

Many enthusiasts for social transformation who fail to appreciate the hegemonic obstacles to achieving social transformation and who also fail to appreciate the need for a civic literacy approach to service learning handicap service learning. Also, faculty who advocate social transformation impose their social and political agenda upon their students. This presents the problem of appearing to violate the institutional and pedagogical principle of liberal neutrality. Flouting or ignoring this principle can result in alienating students whose perspectives differ from that of their professor and even invites the disapproval of the college or university itself. I shall explain and defend what I call the civic literacy approach to service learning, which, I believe, provides a possible solution to the dilemma of the charity and the social transformation approaches to service learning. I believe the civic literacy approach can help to socially transform not only individuals but educational institutions themselves.

This line of analysis will, I hope, be strengthened by drawing upon the civic republican or what I call the liberal or progressive communitarian tradition that sees the self as sourced in community. Illustrative of this approach is the perhaps overused phrase "it takes a village to raise a child." The liberal communitarian view challenges privatized approaches to values by maintaining that individuals are grounded in their essential sociality and that individuals can attain true authenticity and self-fulfillment through community engagement. A healthy community is the only route to self-fulfillment. Second, this approach challenges instrumental reason by suggesting that we must reassert the role of civically engaged individuals in arriving at an understanding and enumeration of social purposes founded not on scientific and technological priorities, but on humane values concerning what promotes the good of community and the rights of individuals.

Finally, I believe we are approaching a crossroads within higher education itself. Service learning has the potential to help higher education become an authentic community partner, serving as a resource for helping members of communities improve community life. But, at the same time, higher education is vulnerable to being co-opted by the very forces the pedagogy of service learning is capable of addressing. Two challenges in particular must be examined. One is the already referenced tendency of the service-learning movement itself to be limited to charity approaches. To be sure, there is great value in promoting an ethic of service among our youth and college students. However, it is, in my opinion, unconscionable for institutions of higher education to contain service learning in this way, given the manifold social problems we are facing.

Second, increasing pressures from the business community to channel educational energies into certain forms of workforce development is challenging the service-learning movement just as it is growing. Of course, it is important that colleges and universities provide work-relevant education and training. However, this is not all that higher education is about. We should be educating our students to play an important role in civic life, again through activities such as service learning, and helping our students to be more than work ready (or as work ready as one can be through obtaining a college degree). Part of the educational experience of civic development should include providing students with the kind of critical perspective to examine, not only their own individual purposes and goals, but to be able to scrutinize the social and economic purposes of society and to be equipped with the means necessary to be able to work to improve society.

Higher education's score card is not good in responding to these matters. Not only have our four-year institutions conspired with a very traditional approach to education in encouraging students to pursue degrees for which there are limited employment opportunities, but mandarin professors also have continued to conspire in an educational system that has promoted forms of scholarship in which professors gain lifelong employment through producing obscure articles relevant only to their academic peers. Also, many faculty are fundamentally mis-educating students through traditional pedagogical efforts emphasizing the acquisition of fact over critical thinking and through the hidden classroom of passive learning. Consequently, students are educated to fit into the workforce but without the civic skills essential to address economic injustice in the university and the society at large. Of course, the pedagogy of service learning has emerged as a correction of this process, but enthusiasm for this movement must not obscure the dominance of traditionalism within higher education itself, traditionalism that resists this kind of innovation in the interests of supporting the status quo.

Overall, I have an ambitious task before me. I am attempting to defend a particular critical populist approach to service learning and civic literacy, to ground this in a particular social philosophy, and to critique certain hegemonic tendencies of education that would co-opt the approach I am taking. This is a difficult task, but one that I believe is extremely important to take on at this particular time.

2

The Concept of the Civil Society and Weak and Strong Democracy

There has been considerable discussion of late concerned with a desire to promote a more civil society. Many adherents of service learning have advocated volunteerism as a means by which we might develop and sustain a more civil society. One of the problematic aspects of the coupling of the concept of civil society with volunteerism is the lack of clarity about these two concepts.

Two meanings of the concept of "civil" need to be distinguished. First, "civil" can mean "of or relating to the state or its citizenry," as in the "civilized society." The second meaning is "adequate in courtesy and politeness," as in "mannerly." These two meanings have become confused in the discussion over promoting a civil society. Adherents of promoting a civil society, I believe, intend the first meaning, but lapse into the second meaning when they consider what steps need to be taken to promote a civil society. How does this happen?

It happens mainly by our tendency to view our society in privatized terms. Somehow we feel that if we would just treat one another in a more courteous and respectful way—that is, be civil in the second sense—we will be a civilized society in the first sense. But this is hardly the case. We can be quite decent to each other as individuals and still support a social system that is uncivil in the other sense. For example, the South in the 1950s was in many respects a very civil place in the sense of people behaving toward each other in a very mannerly and courteous way. The South was known for its hospitality. However, as a racially segregated society, an entire class or ethnic group was denied the most basic requirements of a civilized society in the other sense. Blacks were educated in inferior schools, condemned mainly to work at low paying jobs, especially as sharecroppers. They had to sit in the back of buses, use separate rest rooms, and drink from their own water fountains. They could not eat in white restaurants or spend the night in white hotels and motels. They were discouraged from voting, in many cases even denied the right to vote through the use of complex voter registration tests they had to pass in order to be able to vote. It is ironic that a society known for its gentility and grace was so uncivilized.

Clearly some people have a more conservative concept of the civil society as one in which respect and courtesy are manifest. This is a very privatized view that attributes social problems, such as poverty, racism, and crime, to the failure of individual character. On the assumption that this view is faulty, upholding this attitude can only make matters worse. This view tends to encourage forms of civic education that create a privatized social analysis. But if the problems of society are due not to individual failure but to systemic problems of the political economy, then the more we adhere to the individual view, the fewer human resources we have to find fundamental solutions to our vast social problems.

If, then, we intend the first sense of "civic," we need to ask what we mean by a "civilized society,"since we must mean more than a society that is composed of courteous and respectful citizens. The unexpressed assumption here, I believe, is the concept of a society that functions, not as a group of individuals, but as a citizenry. The earmark of such a society is one in which individuals in some sense understand their identity in terms of the good of all. That is, the citizenry of an authentically democratic society understand that we not only seek personal fulfillment as individuals but we find meaning in and through our commitment to others in sustaining a commonwealth, to adopt a term from Harry Boyte. Boyte (1989) writes:

In much of American history, this strong and active understanding of citizen involvement was expressed through the language, vision, and concept of "the commonwealth." The word suggested an ideal: a commonwealth was a self-governing community of equals concerned about the general welfare—a republican or democratic government, where citizens remained active throughout the year, not simply on Election Day. And commonwealth also brought to mind the touchstone or common foundations, of public life—the basic resources and public goods of a community over which citizens assumed responsibility and authority. (pp. 4–5)

A society constituted of something more than citizens committed to an interpersonal morality in which individuals treat one another with respect is a society understood as a commonwealth. It is one in which individuals work to create a society that promotes and sustains the common good.

Assuming, then, this is what we should be seeking to promote in the name of the "civil society," how do we promote such a society? What are the means by which we can achieve a society in which people function as a commonwealth? Here Boyte is instructive. He maintains that such a society needs to promote effective citizen action and "to *guide* and frame action with integrative concepts and a clear, if flexible and evolving, set of public values and purposes" (p. 5). Although this is an abstract statement, its intent is clear enough. To attain a commonwealth, a truly civil society, we need to create and sustain a society in which people function as effective citizens committed to public values and purposes.

This approach to society contrasts with a more conservative view that understands citizenship as mainly exercising voting rights and displaying patriotism. Ironically, this concept of citizenship is often associated with the more privatized concept of "civil." The commonwealth sense, however, enjoins us to consider our role as citizens as an active one in which we, as individuals, achieve fulfillment in and through our commitment to the public good.

In these terms the means of achieving commonwealth involve promoting civic virtue, or, in my terms, civic literacy. But again, it is a particular understanding of civic virtue. We need to uphold those mechanisms and institutions that foster the attainment of those qualities of character necessary to create and sustain democratic communities. I discuss this concept of virtue in a later chapter. Suffice it to say that the civil society calls for individuals committed to serving the common good in ways that respect the autonomy of individuals.

If this is the kind of civil society we want to achieve, then clearly we need to do more than encourage people to be respectful and courteous. We need to create a society that not only honors individuals, but promotes equality of opportunity for individuals. Such a society will advocate popular sovereignty. It also will strive to create an economy that serves not only individual purposes but public and democratic purposes as well.

This concept of the civil society serves as a normative frame of reference for understanding civic virtue. It also suggests a direction for the role of service. Clearly, we should promote those forms of service that enable us to create commonwealth. This implies that service is richer and deeper than volunteerism, which is often the form of service advocated as a way to promote a civil society. While it is important that we promote a spirit of volunteerism in our society, volunteerism itself can be counter to the goals of commonwealth. This is the case because volunteerism connotes a form of privatized and individualized response to our human and social problems. Individuals who bring food to the soup kitchen, visit the elderly, or participate in a fundraiser to support medical research are to be commended for their volunteerism. However, we must not promote this form of service as the exclusive means for achieving the civil society in the commonwealth sense. It is highly unlikely that these forms of service will accomplish this purpose. This is not to say that volunteerism will not help individuals to grow morally. Quite to the contrary, volunteerism is a great way to help people become reconnected to their community and to begin to outgrow egoistic lifestyles. Nevertheless, volunteerism, because of its individualistic and privatized response to human and social problems, is not a form of service that will create the civic virtues appropriate to achieving commonwealth. Indeed, advocating volunteerism as the essential way to promote the civil society, because of its individualized nature, may have the opposite effect of reinforcing individualized and privatized understandings of society in accord with the more conservative view of the civil society. Instead of seeing poverty as a problem of the public, one may tend to see poverty as an individual problem. Creating commonwealth requires that we engage in forms of service that promote public solutions to social problems.

The commonwealth concept of the civil society is a critical concept for this book. I believe that service, especially in the academic context, is a very promising institutional means of promoting commonwealth, the civil society. And I believe that certain forms of service are more appropriate for securing the civic virtues necessary for commonwealth. Unfortunately, it is all too easy to lose one's way in this kind of discussion because of the privatistic influences on our thinking.

Examining two very different interpretations of democracy that undergird our thinking reveals how our thought is shaped by these influences. The commonwealth tradition is representative of strong democracy, whereas the more privatistic viewpoint associated with the interpersonal understanding of the civil society is derived from the weak democracy tradition. In the remainder of this chapter, I wish to attempt to clarify these two concepts, because I shall draw upon them in developing a critique of non-commonwealth forms of service and civic literacy and in attempting to sustain the thesis that the commonwealth view of service and civic literacy represents the framework for achieving a truly civil society.

A significant body of literature (Barber, 1984, 1992; Bellah et al., 1985, 1991; Boyte, 1989; Boyte and Karii, 1996; Giarelli, 1988; Lappé, 1989; Lappé and Du Bois, 1994; Pratte, 1988a, 1988b; Putnam, 1993, 1995a; Rimmerman, 1997b; Sandel, 1982, 1996, 1996, March; Sullivan, 1982,

1996; Taylor, 1991, 1992; and Wood, 1988) has recently been published explaining and defending a populist understanding of citizenship, a "strong democracy."[1]   Historically, the Kettering Foundation issued an important document, *Civic Declaration: A Call for a New Citizenship* (1994), coordinated by Harry Boyte, Benjamin Barber, and Will Marshall. This document calls unequivocally for a renewed emphasis on civic democracy, what Barber calls strong democracy and Boyte the commonwealth tradition. The document states:

The New Citizenship seeks a return to government of and by as well as for the people, a democracy whose politics is our common public work: where citizens are as prudent in deliberation as we expect our representatives to be; where public problem solving takes the place of private complaint; where all give life to liberty, and rights are complemented by the responsibilities that make them real. A citizen democracy turns blame of others into self-reliance and mutual aid, It transforms passive clients and consumers into active agents of change in our communities, the nation, and the world. It seeks the return of authority from unaccountable structures to the public and to community and civic associations, and the renewal of government and civic institutions alike as sites for public work. (p. 6)

The New Citizenship or civic democracy viewpoint contrasts with a "weak democracy." Weak democracy basically sees the democratic process as subservient to enlightened self-interest. In contrast, strong democracy subordinates individual interests to the common good. I first discuss weak democracy and the implications for civic education.

WEAK DEMOCRACY

Weak democracy emphasizes the role of democracy as ensuring that there are maximal opportunities for individuals to find self-fulfillment independent of government and assumes a view of the autonomous individual, or as Bellah and associates (1985) phrase it, "ontological individualism," that is, the view that individuals are the fundamental reality. Weak democracy relegates the democratic process to that of serving utilitarian individual interests, that is, maximizing aggregate individual preferences. Other social goals, as elaborated by social constituencies, become the driving values. These goals can range from promoting social conservative values of primacy of the family, patriotism, and corporate capitalism, or social liberal values of instrumental reason, individual autonomy, or even social justice.

There are several versions of weak democracy: the neoconservative view, the instrumentalist view, the traditionalist view and the social justice view. I want briefly to describe these views, but I shall treat them in more detail in subsequent chapters as I relate these views to approaches to service learning and to civic literacy.

In terms of the social conservative version, weak democracy regards civic participation as a matter of understanding one's role as a citizen of a country. It stresses the importance of understanding how the government works and promotes the cultivation of patriotism among the young. This view is characteristic of the approach to ethics and civic education, especially in the early school years. But lest we dismiss this as merely an approach of elementary education, we must recognize that this view, along with its philosophical underpinnings, is characteristic of a significant body of social conservative thinking in our society. This typically is the view of democracy behind the more privatized concept of the civil society.

The second view of civic education is the consumerist view. This view often is espoused by those who teach social science. Civic education consists of teaching students the basics of how the government works. This tends to be a protectionist approach that sees citizens as playing a passive role consisting mainly of trips to the ballot box and construes political noninvolvement as a good thing and a sign of satisfaction with the way things are.

Certainly, it is important that people are educated in the civic process. This includes understanding the nature of federal, state, and local government. But that is at best a necessary condition of being civically educated. It is far from sufficient. It is particularly in its failure to help people understand how to work effectively at the community level that the social science form of civic education can be faulted. Such an approach can lead to further civic alienation. It can do so through reinforcing the view that the civic process is one in which experts carry on the business of democracy. Students may get the idea that if they want to participate in the democratic process they can do so through being informed about social issues and voting or they can consider running for public office.

There are two other more liberal views of weak democracy. The first is the view that civic education consists mainly of promoting individual autonomy and strengthening the ability of individuals to exercise their free choices in what is presumed will be in the best interests of all concerned. The role of education for this view is to promote individual autonomy, to help students acquire the ability to think critically, and to make wise decisions in terms of their enlightened self-interest. The liberal defense of education as one that promotes the growth of individuals through liberal arts education is at the heart of this view. This approach, it is believed, will, in the long run, lead to social improvement on the assumption that the educational process is a gradual enlightening process. The failure to appreciate the extent to which education, in the name of liberal education, in reality educates young people to fit into the political economy is one of the immediate problems with this approach. Rather than gradually improving society through a liberal arts education, we find that, in some sense, problems of our society have grown worse. This should not happen if the claims of traditionalism were true.

Justice approaches to civic literacy epitomizes the other weak democracy view. In this view, the civically educated individual is one who is imbued with a strong sense of social justice. It assumes the weak democracy contractarian theory that it is in our self-interest to maximize equality. The problem with this approach is its adversarial philosophy that operates from a zero-sum perspective. It pits the haves against the have-nots and assumes the we are all fighting over a limited piece of economic pie. This approach fails to recognize that there may be deeper values associated with our purposes in life.

STRONG DEMOCRACY

Strong democracy concedes a greater role to the democratic process than mainly upholding individual rights and providing a process by which the common good can be served. This is the commonwealth view. It is generally founded on some version of liberal or progressive communitarianism, although Boyte does not agree with this. He seems to have a fundamental belief in popular sovereignty.

The liberal communitarian view rejects ontological individualism by maintaining that individuals can only find fulfillment in and through society. This view emphasizes the importance of creating social capital and a strong populist civic infrastructure. It sees the democratic process as providing a mechanism not only to protect individual rights but to constrain individual rights in the interests of the common good.

From a populist approach, the weak democratic theories of neo-conservativism, instrumental reason, and the justice model are profoundly undemocratic. They tend to reinforce political cynicism, elite power, and, when taught in schools, they contribute to the reproduction of civically disengaged students. They do this by fueling the already widely held belief that government does not represent the people. For example, many social commentators have observed that the populace sees government as something that politicians engage in; whereas the public sees itself as having a marginal role in the political process. Ross Perot took advantage of this by characterizing the government as a process that does not represent the interests of the people. Perot avoids acknowledging the extent to which corporate America has profited by our governmental policies and that, in fact, he has become a billionaire through the manipulation of business in ways made possible by the very government he criticizes. Having said this, it must be acknowledged that Perot has touched a sensitive nerve in his critique of big government.

Of course, Perot is not the only person to have accumulated great wealth by manipulating our political economy. While there has been a slight decrease in the middle class over the past fifteen years, we have seen an increase in the income of the wealthiest Americans who control over 49% of the wealth. A host of economic factors has contributed to this wealth. Not the least of these are policies that permit large corporate mergers, leverage buy-outs, corporate downsizing, the ability to outsize manufacturing in Third World countries, and the ability to invest profits from these activities in the stock market. Civic education that fails to enable students to understand the connection between "politics" and the "economy" has failed its purpose.

From the strong democracy perspective, a narrow approach to teaching civic understanding in the schools may reinforce civic disconnection rather than promote growth or development in civic understanding. How does this happen? A couple of forces are at work here. A great deal has been written about the reproductive role of education. Through the hidden curriculum students, while being taught the value of equality of opportunity, are educated in such a way that they fail to gain the critical understanding of society necessary to help them begin to work for social change. A narrow form of civic education reinforces this uncritical approach by teaching students a view of history that focuses on the accomplishment of important heroes and "great figures," thereby creating the impression that ordinary people are not all that important to social change. Additionally, students are not provided with tools of social and political analysis and end up typically adopting the view that events take place outside of the control of ordinary people. Add to this the fact that we create the impression that young people are not all that important to the "real" world and that we would just as soon prolong adolescence as long as possible; students do not feel valued or that they have much of a role to play in changing the nature of society.

These traditionalist forms of civic education serve to reinforce the sense of civic disenfranchisement among the citizenry. As I stated in Chapter 1, many people have little political hope or imagination about what can be done at the local level to effect political change. This attitude is doubtless linked to the traditional view, because many people do not even consider community problem solving to be "political." For them, "political activity" means running for office and getting people elected.

Of course, "civic education" is not solely to blame for civic disenfranchisement. Whenever people feel that the political process is something from which they are excluded, political cynicism is reinforced. We witnessed this during the 1994 Clinton and Dole presidential campaign, and we have also seen this in past contests. Many people do not believe that the outcome of the presidential election will have any impact on their lives. We must admit, in all candor, that there is some truth in this public perception. Over the past ten years we have experienced a high degree of political gridlock with one party controlling Congress and the other party, the presidency. With this state of affairs, Congress or the President have found it difficult to pass important legislation.

The populist or strong democracy theory places the greatest emphasis on developing and strengthening participatory democracy. To this end, the civic virtues associated with strong democracy are those of having an understanding of one's social embeddedness and a willingness to work in relationship with others in improving community life informed by an understanding of basing decisions and efforts on a sense of the common good.

NOTE

1. I adopt the phrase from Barber (1984), but I use the term "weak democracy" instead of Barber's "thin democracy." I alternatively refer to weak democracy as "procedural liberalism" adopted from Pratte (1988), and "the procedural republic," adopted from Sandel (1996). The procedural republic refers to the democratic decision making process. Philosophical liberalism refers to the foundational aspect of this tradition. I also use the phrase "civic republicanism" as synonymous with "weak democracy." In this case the phrase emphasizes the democratic decision making process. I also use the phrase "the commonwealth tradition" as synonymous with "strong" or "participatory democracy," emphasizing that this form of democracy involves people recognizing that it is in their mutual interests political to work together and make common cause. More controversial, is my view, which I develop in the course of the book, that strong democracy or the commonwealth tradition theoretically can best be supported by "liberal communitarianism," the view that we are essentially social beings and that we must take into consideration those political decisions policies, procedures that serve the common good or good of all, subject to respecting fundamental principles of liberty and fairness. I briefly defend this theory in due course. Finally, Putnam is more recognized in his arguments for the importance of developing "social capital" rather than in discussing the importance of participatory democracy. Nevertheless, he is sympathetic with the civic republican tradition.

3

Service Learning

Widespread support exists for service learning as one of the ways to promote the civic virtues necessary for creating a more civil society. Service learning also can provide a very effective way for developing and promoting institutional engagement and partnership between higher education and the community. Not everyone is familiar with service learning. So before proceeding further with my line of argument, I wish to provide an overview of service learning and examples of this pedagogy.

Service learning, or academically based community service, is a form of learning in which students engage in community service as part of academic course work.[1] The service experiences are connected with the learning outcomes of the course, and there is the opportunity for teacher-guided reflection on the service experience. Typically this teacher-guided reflection occurs with the instructor asking students to keep journals of their service experience. For example, a student who tutors at an elementary school as a community service project might keep a journal in which the experiences at the school are thoughtfully recorded. The college English instructor might regard this as a writing work in progress. Similarly, an instructor might provide classroom opportunities for students to integrate their observations and reflections on their service experience in relation to some of the topics covered in the course. For example, a sociology instructor might have students who are volunteering in a soup kitchen discuss their observations on poverty when this topic is studied in the sociology course.

Although service learning is a relatively "new" pedagogy, an increasing number of colleges and universities throughout the country are developing service-learning programs. It is apparent that we are in the midst of a true higher education service-learning reform movement. According to the National Campus Compact, there are 520 campus compact member colleges involving over 5,000 faculty and over 500,000 students in this initiative. (Kobrin et al., 1996). Many colleges engaged in service learning are not Compact members. Statistics obviously do not tell the whole story. As one who has visited a great number of campuses and participated in countless conferences and done many presentations at colleges and universities on service learning, I have a strong sense of the excitement that faculty and administrators feel about this movement. It is re-energizing teaching and developing strong partnerships between colleges and communities. Certainly, part of the reason for the popularity of service learning lies in its value as a pedagogy, value for students—value for faculty, and value for the institution, value for the community. I shall review some of these values in the following section.

It is important to emphasize that service learning builds upon the very value of service itself. No matter how civically and economically fair a society is, a need always will exist for volunteers to provide direct service to nonprofit or third-sector organizations. People need not only to donate blood, but to volunteer to help support blood centers. Volunteers are needed to work at senior centers and in emergency relief. Rifkin (1995) has emphasized the importance of the "third sector" work, which can not be replaced by technology, as a site for meaningful work in the future. While I have some concerns about how Rifkin would see this work "funded," nevertheless, I agree that this highlights an area of productive work for people who may find themselves with time on their hands and the need to do something meaningful in society.

So long as we have the kind of society that we do, one characterized by extremes of economic inequality and all of the consequential problems associated with inequality, more volunteer work is needed than we can provide. Homeless shelters need people to provide food and to work in kitchens preparing food and serving food. Volunteers are needed to collect, sort, and hand out clothes, furnishings, and other needed goods. Shelters for battered women requires some of the same services. In addition, these shelters need capable people to operate hot-lines and to provide day care. Our public schools need mentors and tutors. Affordable housing is one of our most acute needs. We have a strong need for volunteers to assist in projects, such as Habitat for Humanity, a nationally recognized organization that builds homes for economically disadvantaged families, and to work in inner-city housing renovation projects. Alongside our many environmental problems, volunteers are critically needed to help clean up and beautify our cities. We need people to do conservation work in many of our state and national parks, including trail construction. The urgent need of volunteers to address our many urban and rural problems in the areas of education, housing, environment, and human services continues to grow. This speaks to the value of the AmeriCorps that has provided an army of paid volunteers to provide help in these areas. Most states have AmeriCorps volunteers, which is funded by the Corporation for National Service (CNS). These individuals function like a domestic Peace Corps. They receive a living allowance for working up to thirty hours per week and a post-service benefit after two years to be applied toward educational costs such as tuition. AmeriCorps volunteers engage in public work projects, including tutoring, environmental cleanup, and inner city renovation. Boyte and Kari (1996) see AmeriCorps as contributing to the value of public work. They believe that creation of public work is one of the ways to offset our tendency toward privatization.

Additionally, CNS funds service learning projects through its Learn and Serve Higher Education initiative. In the beginning of CNS in 1992 colleges and universities received funds to start up service-learning programs. In the past few years the Corporation has funded statewide initiatives. In particular, most of the state campus compacts, now numbering twenty-one, have received grants to provide faculty stipends at colleges and universities to integrate service-learning projects into their courses. State campus compacts are part of the National Campus Compact, located in Providence Rhode Island. The state compacts are fee-based membership organizations, and colleges and universities who join the state compacts receive a variety of support services, such as the opportunity to apply for faculty fellow grants. The National Campus Compact has received substantial grants from the Corporation as well as from the Ford Foundation and other sources to promote national service-learning initiatives. One of the most successful of these has been a project spanning a number of years promoting the integration of service into academic courses. The National Compact has provided funds for regional conferences on this topic.

An example of another Corporation funded initiative is the project, "From the Margins to the Mainstream: The Faculty Role," with the Campus Compact National Center for Community Colleges (CCNCCC), directed by Lyvier Conns and located at Mesa Community College in Mesa, Arizona. This initiative provides technical assistance to community colleges to all states except Alaska, who want to develop or expand service-learning projects. For two years I served as one of six mentors providing this technical assistance. During the final year of the project other faculty members at my college, the Community College of Aurora, continue to work in this mentoring capacity. This year I started working on another national project with CCNCCC's, "Two Plus Four Equals Service on Common Ground," that involves seven pairs of community colleges and universities, doing common community projects together. Finally, CNC Learn and Serve (grades) K-12 provides grants to public schools for community service projects, usually distributed through the state departments of education.

Promoting a spirit of volunteerism is often the pathway or route for drawing young people into community involvement (Wuthnow, 1991, and Coles, 1993). Community service is often the age appropriate way for young people to become involved in their communities. It is particularly appropriate at the elementary- and middle-school level of schooling. These young people are not mature enough, nor should we expect them to be, to tackle more complicated community improvement projects. Yet these youngsters can make vital contributions to their community through service.

And we can not expect many of our older students to move beyond an "ethic of service" orientation. So long as the motives for community involvement flow from a spirit of service, we will have achieved a great deal. If only we had more young people involved in their community out of a motive of service, we would be the better for it.

An important way to grow morally is through becoming engaged in service. I have written elsewhere about the importance of service learning as a tool of moral development (D. Lisman, 1996a; J. Boss 1994). One of the biggest challenges that we face in attempting to get students to move beyond relativistic, egoistic, and apathetic attitudes is that students do not as a rule give up these attitudes even in the face of criticism. In over twenty years of teaching ethics, I have seen few students give up these viewpoints because of any criticisms that are raised against these positions. However, I have seen students genuinely affected by their service experiences. Although this does not always happen, students, through providing service to others, began to realize the importance of other human beings. They realize that the interests, opinions, and values of others are important to take into consideration as they consider how they should act and live. By any reasonable concept of ethics, such students are beginning to grow as moral beings.

Thus, service is important both for our society and for the individuals who perform the service. And throughout this book, I should never be taken as being critical of the "ethic of service" in this sense. I only express concern about the appropriation of this spirit of service for other purposes. We must be alert to the question of service for what purpose?

THE VALUE OF SERVICE LEARNING

Skeptics about the value of service learning for higher education always have been and will exist. As I discuss below, some of that skepticism is founded in a more traditional view of education in which it is believed that the most important value is to teach students certain academic skills and concepts and to prepare them for the workforce. Historically, a conflict between education for democracy and education for the workforce has existed. This tension is reflected in the service-learning movement. I shall have more to say about this tension in later chapters. Let us first review some of the more obvious reasons why service learning is good for education.

Value as a Pedagogy

Service learning as a pedagogy has two important components. One is its contribution to a learning-oriented pedagogy as opposed to a teaching pedagogy. The other is its contribution as a form of experiential education. Recently Barr and Tagg (1995) have advocated the need to develop a student-learning pedagogy as opposed to a teacher-directed orientation. This approach is in accord with cooperative forms of learning where students work in groups as teams. It also is in accord with problem-based learning and case-study approaches. But service-learning stands out because of the action-oriented nature of learning.

At the same time that service learning was being championed in the mid-1980s as a way to help reconnect students with the community, writers began to talk about service learning as a form of experiential education. Dewey is often cited as a precursor of service learning, with his insistence on the importance of learning by doing (1938, 1956). Over the years professors scattered around the country have had students volunteering in the community as part of their educational experience. More often than not, however, student volunteerism has occurred as an activity of social or service clubs, and these experiences have not been connected to academic work. Additionally, many forms of experiential education have existed prior to service learning, including apprenticeships, internships, and cooperative experiences. Apprenticeships are usually vocational training programs in which a student studies and learns on the job, such as in the training of electricians or machinists. In higher education, experiential education has taken the form of internships, which usually consist of unpaid work occurring as a capstone experience, such as when a criminal justice student works at the city court. Cooperative experiences are typically paid-work experiences that are tied to the course work in a particular course of vocational study, such as medical transcription. All these forms of experiential learning have been utilized in vocational training. What has been relatively new about service learning is its focus on promoting an "ethic of service" and the inclusion of the service experience as part of the course work of any course, vocational or nonvocational.

The vocational component may still be associated with service learning. For example, in a criminal justice program, a student may do a shorter community service project as part of a beginning criminal justice course, with the internship occurring at the end of the program. Although often resistant to integrating service learning into such programs, many instructors are discovering the vocational value to having students do a service experience at the beginning of the program. Through the service experience, students often can discover early in the program whether this vocation meets their needs. In addition, introducing a service experience at the beginning of the program enables the students also to get a grounding in the "service" dimensions of the program. As an example, students in our college's criminal justice and paralegal programs have provided informational presentations on legally-related matters to low-income family members at our campus-based family center. In addition to applying what they are learning, these students are developing an important sense of the service dimension of their work.

Including service learning in liberal arts and science courses brings not only the added benefit of experiential or applied learning, but also allows students too take advantage of their service experience to explore careers. For example, as a result of doing a service experience at an elementary school for my ethics class, one of my students, decided to become a public school teacher rather than an accountant.

The distinguishing mark of service learning in this regard is that it is a pedagogy, a form of teaching and learning that attempts to connect the subject matter and the student with the real world through having the student volunteer in the community, often in governmental institutions and community-based organizations, such as public schools, homeless shelters, hospitals, shelters for the protection of battered women, and senior centers. However, when focusing on the value of service learning as a pedagogy, attention is usually directed to the concept of experiential learning.

As a form of experiential learning, students are encouraged to seek out service experiences that bear some relationship to the subject being studied in the classroom. For example, a student might be studying the topic of poverty in sociology. As an aspect of learning more about this topic, the student might volunteer at a homeless shelter. Perhaps the student will serve in the food line or wash dishes in the kitchen. While at the homeless shelter, the student might avail himself or herself of the opportunity to become acquainted with some of the homeless people who come to the shelter.

Kolb (1984) provides an important analysis of the nature of experiential learning. According to Kolb, experiential learning involves having some kind of practical learning experience and reflection on that experience. Through the reflective process a theory or conceptual analysis is developed to understand the experience better, and then the theory is tested in experience. Take a mundane example. A person might decide to find the best route to and from work. This person might compare time, mileage, traffic patterns among several possible routes. As a result of driving these routes and doing these comparisons, this individual might conclude that a particular route is the best route (the "theory"). Then the individual continues to drive the routes alternatively over a period of weeks to determine finally which is the best route, presumably confirming that the tentatively agreed upon route is the best one.

This concept of "learning" is helpful as far as it goes, but when applied to academically based service learning, more often than not a student may be asked to "test" a concept or idea against practical experience, instead of deriving a concept or theory from practical experience. For example, a student might be asked in a psychology class to determine whether a particular view of self-esteem is mirrored by the people they come into contact with in their service experience. Students might accordingly revise their concept in light of their service experience and arrive at a more subtle concept or deeper understanding of the concept as a result of applying the concept in the real world.

Sometimes, a student may not have a task so teacher-directed. The professor instead may ask the student to be on the look out for subject-relevant material in the context of the service experience. And here the student, of course, might have at his or her disposal a variety of concepts or topics from the course to examine in the light of the service experience. A psychology student might examine the concept of self-esteem while tutoring in the public school, or a chemistry student might study complex chemical reactions associated with pollution while testing water in a nearby reservoir. These students might keep journals in which they reflect on the relationship of the concept to of self-esteem while serving as a mentor at a public school.

There are other more sophisticated ways in which the student can correlate course content to the service experience, such as problem solving and action research. Suffice it to say for now, that, as an experiential education pedagogy, service learning provides many ways and opportunities for the student to enrich classroom learning or study. It is important that the instructor be intentional and thoughtful about helping direct the student in this regard.

Academia must avoid using the community as a laboratory. Students who subject people at community-based agencies to interviews may cause these interviewees to feel that they are being exploited for the sake of an academic research project. Service leaning can overcome this barrier because of the fact that the student provides service to the community in the context of engaging in research instead of just doing field research. So if the homeless shelter members perceive the student as someone who works there and exhibits concern for the people, the shelter residents are much more likely to be willing to talk to the student. Even then it is important that the student treat the homeless people in a respectful manner and respect their desire for privacy and not be intrusive. The student needs to avoid at all costs conveying to the people served that all the student cares about is doing research. Students usually become involved in the issues and develop and exhibit concern and compassion for people they serve. Therefore, the concern about students coming across as exploitative or insensitive to the situation of the people they are serving is minimal.

Certainly, service learning is a great form of experiential education. Not only does it make the subject "come alive" through real world application, but students become drawn into the context in which they are working. Students, like professors, bring their share of biases into academia. This is particularly true of biases regarding social issues. I noted in the first chapter that we are divided as a society about many of the great social issues of the day, such as poverty, affirmative action, health care, public education, and the environment, to cite but a few of the contested issues. I have argued elsewhere (Lisman, In press) that service learning provides a way by which not only students' biases can be challenged but their irrational attitudes also can be minimized.

The area in which I have the greatest concern is that of engagement with value issues. It is, of course, useful for students to engage in community research, again to be discussed in more detail later, and to apply academic subject matter taught in the classroom to the real world. But the most significant issues which divide us are ethical and social matters. There is only so much that can be done effectively about these issues in the classroom. At worst, the classroom simply becomes a place where the instructor patiently tries to present alternative sides to controversial issues, while many students remain disengaged. At best, students gain information relevant to assessing ethical and social issues, but they frequently do not become engaged with the issues in a way sufficient to affect a change in attitude or value.

Of course, students may not want to change their attitudes or values; nor is it always desirable to try to change their attitudes. Sometimes, they may be on the "right" side. Also, at times students may not be developmentally ready to change their position on an issue. For example, a young student, right out of high school, may still reflect the values of his/her upbringing. This is quite normal. Many of us can recall the painful process of coming to question our home taught values. A change in values does not usually take place over night. With younger students, we can only hope to plant seeds of change.

However, some students are ready to change their viewpoint. Equally, some students are so set in their ways that classroom discussion has little or no impact upon their viewpoint. This is where service learning is useful. Students are thrust into situations of poverty, of women who have been victims of abuse, of a polluted environment. And as they confront these situations in the real world, not only can the student better grasp the relevance of the classroom information, but he or she may find his or her attitudes challenged. The world of pain and suffering, of hope and goodwill beckons the student and challenges him or her to think through controversial issues in terms of confrontation with people directly affected by these issues.

Also a strong case can be made that providing service to others is one of the ways that we begin to create or strengthen a sense of the public. As Matthews (1994) and Palmer (1996) have advocated, a public forms when people work together on common concerns. I have already suggested that one of the sources of our civic erosion is the lack of a sense of the public. We live in a highly privatized society in which many people see very little reason for investing their own personal resources or energies in helping others. But as people grow in their commitment to others through service, a by-product is that attainment of a sense of the public.

Such an important need for strengthening our sense of the public exists (Putnam, 1995a), that I am reluctant to raise criticisms about some views of service, for fear that I will be taken as criticizing the ethic of service itself. So lest I be misunderstood, let me say unequivocally that I am an advocate of the ethic of service. I believe that we need it desperately in our society and that without promoting this ethic or spirit among people in our society, there is little hope that we will move beyond cynical, egoistic, relativistic, and privatized approaches to life and come together as a public and community. However, I am concerned that "service" will be appropriated by interests and educational institutional concerns that result in diluting and distorting service. But more of that later.

Value for Students

Students have discovered that service learning is beneficial in many ways. Some of the research regarding student outcomes will be reviewed. I then discuss some of other student benefits.

Institutions of higher education have widely embraced service learning or the curricular integration of community service because it fundamentally is an effective pedagogy. Related to and in addition to the above remarks, I might share some of the research related to the impact of service learning on students, civically and academically. Jacoby states that "the existing research on service-learning, although much of it focuses on students at the elementary and secondary school levels, has been encouraging" (1996, pp. 322).[2] Service learning has been correlated with an increase in grade-point average and improved academic performance (Greco, 1992; Hannah and Dworkowitz, 1992; Levinson and Felberbaum, 1993; Nelms, 1991). Krehbiel and MacKay (1988) reported that 90 % of student volunteers found service learning as valuable as or more valuable to them than classroom work. This research is supported by that of Crowner (1992) and Miller (1994).

Other studies have found community service to enhance students' moral development (Boss, 1994; Boyd, 1980). Service learning also is effective in building students' self-esteem (Adams, 1993; Driscoll et al., 1996). Recent studies suggest that service learning connected to a specific course can increase students' learning of course content (Boss, 1994; Cohen and Kinsey, 1994; Markus et al., 1993; Miller, 1994; Driscoll et al., 1996). Two studies at Vanderbilt University (Giles and Eyler, 1994) and Alma College (Batchelder and Root, 1994), found that service learning improves grades and the ability to apply course concepts to new situations and, further, that students show increased motivation for learning, social responsibility, and citizenship and civic involvement. Kendrick (1996) has arrived at similar results. Additionally, the Driscoll research at Portland State University (Driscoll et al., 1996) found that service-learning students developed increased self-awareness, awareness of and involvement with community, personal development, sense of service, sensitivity to diversity, and independence in learning.

A recent three-year study from Brandeis University confirms the student outcome trends already commented upon above (Roberts, 1997), although it is a study of middle- and high-school service-learning student outcomes. Seven middle schools and ten high schools in nine states were studied. This research found that service-learning can strengthen civic attitudes, promote volunteer activity, and improve learning in young people. The programs were selected to represent well-designed, fully implemented service-learning programs. All are school-based programs that involve students in regular volunteer service—an average of seventy-seven hours per student—linked to classroom instruction and a formal course curriculum reflection on the service experience.

The interim report describes the program impacts for students who participated during the 1995–96 academic year. The final report for the evaluation will examine longer-term, follow-up outcomes and will be completed in early 1998. Major findings to date include the following: service learning had a positive impact on the civic development of program participants; and participants scored significantly higher on measures of personal and social responsibility, acceptance of cultural diversity, and service leadership as compared to a control group. The service learning programs had a positive impact on measures of educational engagement, aspirations, and achievement. Service-learning students had higher grades in social studies, math and science than the control group and were more likely to want to go to a four-year college. They rated their school experience more positively than did a group of comparison students. The positive impact on school grades was particularly strong for middle school students.

In addition to the academic value of service learning for students, there are a number of other benefits. In the first place, service learning provides students with tools they need in order to succeed in today's workforce. Many educators are concerned that students acquire work readiness skills, such as teamwork, leadership, and critical thinking—the ability to analyze and synthesize information.

Finally, Alexander W. Astin is conducting a comprehensive service-learning study at the Higher Education Research Institute (HERI) of the University of California in partnership with the RAND Corporation. They are studying President Clinton's Learn and Serve America: Higher Education program. This study examines thirty-four different student outcome measures, falling in three general areas: civic responsibility, academic development, and life skills development. Although the study is not complete, there are encouraging preliminary results. Astin (1996) writes: "Among the more interesting specific outcomes favorably affected by service participation are persistence in college, interest in graduate study, critical thinking skills, leadership skills, and commitment to promoting racial understanding" (p. 16).

Teamwork skills can be promoted in a variety of ways through service learning. Students may, for example, work together on a service-learning project, as they do in some of my classes. Students in my ethics classes work together in developing a presentation on an ethical issue, such a poverty or affirmative action. They each are responsible for individual contributions to this presentation and are graded accordingly. The students work together as a team in dividing up research tasks and assigning presentation roles. Students may also work together in a service project and agree to divide tasks in the context of their service experience.

Another example of teamwork in relation to service learning is that students may work together on a community project. Although not a service-learning course, an example of this at the Community College of Aurora involved the ColoradoCorps members. The Colorado Campus Compact had a special AmeriCorps called the ColoradoCorps from 1994–97. ColoradoCorps members provided technical assistance to higher education service learning programs. Community College of Aurora participated in this initiative. During academic year 1996–97, five ColoradoCorps members provided support to the college's service-learning program. One of those activities was the Colorado Campus Compact Leadership minigrant. Several of the ColoradoCorps members developed and implemented an after school mentoring program for middle-school students. It was interesting observing the ColoradoCorps members working together on this as a team in negotiating, planning, implementation, evaluation, and, of course, mentoring. Admittedly, there are other college activities, especially social club activities in which college students gain this kind of teamwork ability. But service learning provides other avenues as well.

Additional examples of teamwork include community development work and community action research. Students can have unparalleled rich experiences in doing this kind of activity. For instance, they might help a local neighborhood group create a community garden. This activity can involve research on what would be the best plants for the garden and what the community members would like to have planted. Not only do students have to work through problems together, but they have the extraordinary opportunity to experience first-hand the power of community-based organizations working together to confront social issues, solve problems, build community assets, and increase civic capacity. As part of this process, the students can experience the same kind growth, which can not be replicated in any other kind of educational experience.

Another important job-relevant skill is critical thinking. Perhaps the least effective way to promote this skill is through the traditional lecture method. Here students mainly serve as passive receptacles of information. At the very least, instructors need to design instructional experiences that enable students to analyze and synthesize information. Community service experience certainly provide many opportunities for students to develop critical thinking skills. Students have to assess the needs of an organization where they are going to conduct a project, and they must assess how a possible project correlates to a course-specific topic or concept they are working on. In addition, the daily practical demands of the project enable students to improve their ability to make decisions. One of the important values in this regard is that making decisions that carry with it the responsibility of consequences to others adds a certain significance or weight to that decision.

Realizing the importance of the community consequences of student work can help students develop their own sense of moral character. As an individual recognizes the impact of others as a result of one's conduct, this can help motivate one to develop greater self-discipline. Of course, we are all by nature human and succumb to temptations and desires, and all have lapses of discipline, whether it is overeating or failing to get enough exercise. Possibly, a lack of self-discipline reflects the sense that one feels that no one cares about what one is doing. The self-help movement exemplifies this weakness. If lack of self-discipline is a product of lack of self-esteem, simply being prodded to improve oneself in a particular respect may bear no fruit. Many of us can relate to this from our failed New Year's resolutions. But in the context of service, which is one way that we may find ourselves making decisions that have consequences for other people, we come to realize that not only are we important to other people and that our actions matter, but we may decide to be more responsible to ourselves not only because it is in our self-interest to do so, but because we believe that what we do matters to others.

Another value is leadership. Service learning enables students in many instances to be in a position of leadership. Students may find themselves leading a group of other college students in a project or serving as mentors to other people through the service experience, such as mentoring middle-schools students in the public schools. A great deal of literature testifies to the value of providing service as a means to growing in leadership. However, sometimes this leadership material reflects an individualistic concept of leadership, which in itself reflects a traditional corporate approach to leadership. Leadership in the context of service learning provides the groundwork for helping promote a sense of community leadership.

Of course, community leadership, in the sense of working in a way to help promote community-based efforts to improve community life, does not necessarily follow from doing service in the community. This is especially the case for service experiences that consist mainly of charitable actions. It is interesting that there is a parallel between the concept of leadership and nature of the service experience. Charitable acts of service are associated with a more individualistic view of leadership, whereas community-service and civic-building service experiences lend themselves to a model of community leadership. I discuss this concept further in a later chapter.

The instructor needs to be sure to design leadership experiences that are gender sensitive. As many of us who teach know, males all too often step forward as self-anointed leaders. I find myself having to be very directive with my students to assure that females also play leadership roles. At times I have instructed my college students as they give reports, that males will not be allowed to be the reporter in a small group session and that males must serve as the recorder of the discussion that goes on in small group discussions. Another valuable aspect of service learning for students is that service learning can enable them to explore careers and to build their resumes. Students in the context of their service experiences can explore career options. I have already mentioned that one of my students, as a result of volunteering in an elementary school, decided that she wanted to become a public school teacher rather than an accountant. Sadly, students are often not exposed to career options as they move through the early years of school. As they find themselves volunteering in a homeless shelter or working at a community-based organization or doing a science project in the community, they get a better sense of what it feels like to be involved in a particular vocation or profession than they do from reading about a career or talking with a career counselor. It also is valuable, of course, for students to explore career possibilities in other ways, such as visiting businesses and conducting interviews. Nevertheless, service-learning experiences afford unique opportunities to explore careers.

Not only can students explore careers through service learning, but they can gain considerable practical experience in a career leading to a job. Getting a job without practical experience is difficult in many careers. Students can obtain this experience through internships. Many career programs, such as criminal justice and social work, have such internships, but they are not available in other areas. For example, if someone wants to be a reporter or a journalist, he or she may not be able to find an appropriate internship, although I would imagine some journalist programs have internships. And there certainly is no internship for someone who wants to become a college professor, except perhaps serving as a graduate teaching assistant. Thus, one can get a foot in the door for careers like these while gaining writing or teaching experience through service. A student can do writing activities for a community-based organization by assisting with the production of a newsletter or other publications about the organization. I mentioned that one of our programs, criminal justice, has students do presentations on a variety of issues helpful to family members at our college family center as part of their service experience. Not only does this provide them with a valuable way to deepen their understanding of the topics they are studying in their criminal justice classes, but it will provide them with teaching experiences should they decide to become a criminal justice professor.

Service learning also can help students enhance their resumes. High school students these days recognize the value of introducing extra-curricular activities as part of a college application. Highly competitive colleges and universities look for students who have a well-rounded education. Many look to see if students are involved in their communities. The same applies to many companies as they consider whether or not to hire a prospective employee. College graduates who have a record of significant community service experience increase their likelihood of being hired. And of course, as stated above, a student who also can include in the resume that some of this service experience has enabled the student to perform tasks that are directly relevant to the job being sought may give him or her an advantage over another candidate without this experience.

Students may also use their service-learning experience as a way to work on a personal issue. Students often deal with a host of personal issues, depending on their level of development, age, and the circumstances of their personal life. A student may be dealing with faith issues or a career decision, or may feel alienated from parents, or may have to face the death of a grandparent. Older students may be working through the effects of a divorce or of having been involved in an abusive relationship.

Students often select service-learning projects that enable them to deal with these kinds of personal issues. I have had students volunteer in a senior care facility or a Meals on Wheels program in order to work through having had a grandparent die or confront their guilt because a grandparent is in a nursing home. I have seen people volunteer in AIDS and homosexual support centers because they are dealing with the issue of a friend or relative being HIV-infected or being gay or lesbian. One student volunteered in a hospice because she was dealing with having lost one of her parents. I recall one case of a student who simply did not like older people. As a result of her service experience in which she worked in a Meals on Wheels program, she developed a friendship with an elderly woman. She continued this friendship after her service project. I certainly would not advocate that in working with students to develop academic discipline-appropriate service experience they should only focus on "personal issues." But this is, indeed, an appropriate consideration. I would not necessarily have students identify a "personal issue" they want to work on in their service project. This is unnecessarily intrusive, and students may not wish to disclose their personal concerns. However, this kind of information often comes out in journals and in reflection sessions.

Another benefit to students is that service learning helps build self-esteem. This need is particularly appropriate for community colleges that serves nontraditional students. Many of these students enter college with multiple family concerns, or they may have come into the community college after having failed in their academic attempts at a four-year college or university. In many cases, because community college have open enrollment policies, these students enroll there as the only affordable point of entrance into higher education. They have not had many successful experiences in education and may exhibit little self-confidence. In my own teaching, I have often felt that one of my primary goals is to help increase students' self-confidence. In addition to the research listed above, there is strong evidence through student journals and anecdotal information from faculty across the country that students grow in self-confidence as they engage in community work. I have written elsewhere (Lisman, 1987) that in one sense we contribute to a lack of self-confidence in our youth by not providing them with ways to do meaningful activities. Service learning addresses this gap, and although many students resist the idea of engaging in service learning because of their busy lives, those who do participate frequently cite in their journals how they have grown in self-confidence through their activities. For example, one of my students wrote that she felt useful for the first time in serving as a companion to an elderly person.

A final benefit of service learning for students is that it motivates them to take ownership in their learning. Too often classroom learning is passive. Students are regarded as the passive vessels which faculty fill with knowledge. But we all know that knowledge is not just there to be absorbed as a sponge does liquid. Rather, we are active participants in the social construction of knowledge. Students begin to grow as learners when they grasp that they are important players in this construction of knowledge. As students discern through their projects in the community that they are responsible not only to show up and provide service, but actually to come up with solutions to everyday problems, they begin to realize that they have an important role to play to contributing to community work. Moreover, as they relate their community work to course content, applying their community work as a tool in contributing to their understanding of this academic content, they can began to sense the importance of their role in the creation of knowledge.

Value for Faculty

Less research has been conducted on faculty outcomes in relation to service learning. It is, of course, logical to infer that faculty who are committed to helping their students learn have been quite satisfied with having courses that include academically based community service. The Driscoll (Driscoll et al.,1996) study found that community service teaching experiences have contributed to the increase of faculty service-learning research, conference presentations, and publications. Additionally Hesser, (1995) in a study at Augsburg College, found that 83 % of the forty-eight faculty respondents went on record to the effect that the service-learning version of their courses was strengthening the quality of learning relative to what they had been doing in the past.

I have worked with two national service-learning projects, the American Association of Community Colleges' Learn and Serve Higher Education (1994–97) and the previously mentioned Campus Compact National Center for Community Colleges, Learn and Serve Higher Education Grant "From the Margins to the Mainstream: The Faculty Role" (1995–97). I served as mentor coordinator of the AACC project, involving six mentors from five colleges working with ten mentee colleges who received grants to develop and expand service-learning programs. And I mentioned I have just completed two of three years as a faculty mentor in the "Margins" project in which five other faculty members and I have served as regional representatives assisting community colleges to develop and expand service-learning programs, my region being the Rocky Mountain area. This work has involved me with dozens of colleges, several over a three-year period, and the collective work of these two projects has included over a hundred community colleges. The anecdotal and qualitative research and evaluation overwhelmingly support the above findings.

For faculty committed to helping students learn, the pedagogical effects of service learning benefit them as well. As faculty find that applied learning enables students to learn course material more effectively, to see the relevance of their learning to society, this improves both learning and teaching and makes them more satisfying.

A related benefit is that when done well, a service-learning course is simply more interesting for the teacher and student. Students write more interesting papers and respond more enthusiastically to issues. The classroom becomes a much more interesting place for learning. To give one example, a couple of students did a presentation on gay issues in my ethics class. They volunteered in a gay rights organization and invited a gay individual to talk to the class as part of their presentation. Because they had struck up a good rapport with this gay person in the context of their service work, the individual was quite willing to come and address the class and consequently made the issue come to life. I was astonished to learn when reading the reports of these two service-learning students, that they actually were opposed to extending social rights to homosexuals, such as permitting homosexual marriages and providing additional protections against job discrimination. Given their resistance to homosexuality, it is highly unlikely that without service learning the opposing viewpoint would have been so forcefully presented as it was by the gay visitor.

Value for Educational Institutions

An excellent way for a school to build good relations with the community is through having a service-learning program. As I have written elsewhere (Lisman, 1996), service learning was the mechanism that helped get our own college more involved in the life of our community. For example, as a result of our service-learning program, we become more sensitized to the problem of homelessness and the needs of low-income families. Consequently, our college developed a family center to help respond to these needs. We also have developed a strong partnership with our local school district through a Kellogg-funded project in which college students mentor middle-school students working with them in service projects through a special topics sociology course. There have been numerous spin-offs and other collaborative activities between our college and the school district as a result of this initiative.

Value for the Community

In some respects a college is invisible. It exists in the community like a hospital, similarly, providing a service. But often the college is not regarded as a significant ally in helping to improve community life. In fact the traditional town/gown relationships have even been at times adversarial. Town members see "transient" college students coming into their town or community for nine month durations, often engaging in questionable behavior, such as having drunken parties. No doubt some community members resent college students and faculty because they feel that these people are participating in an elite process of education as a means of social mobility to which they are denied because they do not have the wherewithal or the credentials to enroll in the college. We must be on guard against portraying elitist attitudes in our service work.

Still other community members at the lower end of the economic ladder have suffered educational failure in the public schools and are intimated by and resentful of the local college. They see this institution as an alien presence, perpetuating privilege and affluence for others, and they have no conception as to how they might access this intimidating institution. Even community colleges do not escape this kind of negativity.

Service learning, when done well, can be a means of bridging the town-/gown gap. The community comes to regard the college students in a more positive light. And as service-learning projects link up to community-based organizations and social agencies that serve low-income individuals, the college is seen as more "user friendly." Service-learning activities can even be designed in such a way as to provide opportunities for low-income individuals to access the college. Low-income individuals with whom students work, could, for example, be asked to come and talk to a class about their concerns with the community. All of this, of course, must be done with great care to assure that these individuals are treated with respect. It is also important that the college work to find ways to help individuals become more empowered to overcome difficult circumstances, a subject of a later chapter in this book.

Service-learning activities can lead to the development of projects to assist members in addressing urban and rural problems and in developing projects to improve community life; this constitutes one of the greatest potential benefit to the community is that. I discuss this subject further in Chapter 7. As an example, some community service projects have involved working with community-based organizations or neighborhood groups to create community gardens. Such a project accomplishes many positive results. It provides an activity that can bring community members together; it builds trust among community members which can lead to further conversation, plans, and projects to improve community life; and it provides fun activities and enjoyable produce.

MODELS OF SERVICE LEARNING AND WHERE DO WE GO FROM HERE?

As I mentioned above, there is a certain elegance about service, in the sense of providing service to community. It is a tool of spiritual, personal, and public growth. This is reflected in the work of Sigmon (Sigmon et al., 1996). He says, "The notion of Service-Learning is nothing new in human experience. It happens to be a label given to the coming together of these two notions: our innate desire to contribute and our desire to learn and grow as human beings" (p. 92). No doubt many faculty and others support service learning out of compassionate motives. And there is nothing wrong with this, as I have indicated, insofar as one is interested in promoting a spirit of volunteerism and an ethic of service. Service-learning clearly can contribute to moral growth. (Boss, 1994; Lisman, 1994). However, leaving aside the personal, moral, and spiritual value of service, service learning has been embraced by institutions of higher education for societal purposes as well. It is apparent there are different outcomes associated with service. Some people support and engage in service learning mainly because they are committed to doing acts of charity—good deeds as it were. This view has been criticized for being content with providing direct service to the less fortunate at the expense of not working to address and eliminate the root causes of many problems that are recipients of such direct service, such as soup kitchens and homeless shelters.

Others engage in service learning out of a desire to achieve social transformation, to create a society of greater equality. Advocates of this view of service learning hope that as students become involved in service activities, they will, as a result of their service experiences combined with critical reflection, come to adopt a deeper understanding of the systemic causes of such social problems as poverty and racism and will be motivated to work for social and political change. This view has been criticized for violating the principle of liberal neutrality associated with our educational institutions. Professors and teachers have an educational institutional obligation to assure that contrasting views of issues be presented and that students not be pressured into adopting a particular viewpoint. The professors who want to see their students engage in activities aimed at promoting greater social justice may be violating this principle of liberal neutrality. This approach to service learning is faced with the challenge of justifying a justice approach to service that respects liberal neutrality.

Finally, many are interested in service learning out of a desire to promote greater civic responsibility. This perspective assumes that the greatest value of service learning is that it not only involves students in their communities, but that they acquire greater civic virtue in the process. This approach has been criticized as at best having an unclear concept of civic literacy or at worst trying to get students to take on certain civic values that have proved ineffective in our society. I shall attempt to clarify this concept in a later chapter as I defend the commonwealth or citizen democracy concept of civic literacy.

With all of these different approaches to service learning, we are confronting something of a crisis concerning its purposes (Kahne and Westheimer, 1996, May). We must clarify the conceptual foundations of service learning and what we are attempting to accomplish. Jacoby and associates (1996) is useful in providing an overview of the service-learning movement, but this book reflects the lack of any unity about why institutions of higher education should be doing service learning. A constant tension exists between the use of service learning as a mechanism to improve academic learning and its use to improve social conditions. While there are continuous efforts to confer academic legitimacy on service learning, fostered by the good work of the *Michigan Journal of Community Service Learning* and the American Association of Higher Education monograph series with discipline-specific volumes (Zlotkowski, 1996), some have questioned whether service learning's civic and community-development mission is being co-opted by academic legitimization (Mattson and Shea, 1997). I attempt to sort through these issues and provide a grounding of service learning in the strong democracy tradition. Bearing in mind that some have criticized this kind of civic grounding of service learning as undermining its community development dimension (Harkavy, 1996a), I attempt to show that a more robust concept of the strong democracy view of service learning requires a strong community development component.

As I have indicated, I discuss these different approaches to service learning in the context of civic literacy. I indicate that as a matter of fact, these views are all associated with particular views of democracy, education, and concepts of civic literacy. I attempt to show that the commonwealth civic literacy model provides a way to embrace values of the charity and social justice models, while also providing a more comprehensive framework for linking education to the community. In the following chapters, I lay out four views of society and government/politics that are associated with four different views of the role of education, pedagogy, and service learning. I defend the final or fourth view, the strong democracy, or participatory democracy, view. In the final chapters, I discuss what higher education and service learning will look like in the service of this view and provide examples of this view.

The four views that I take up in greater detail in the following chapters include the following: First, I discuss the neoconservative libertarian theory of society, which is associated with an indoctrinative view of civic education, at least in the early years of youth development, and a volunteerist view of service learning. Second, the consumerist or democratic elitist view of politics, emphasizing instrumental reason and scientism and having a social and informational transmission view of education. This view supports an experiential education model of service learning. Third, I discuss the more radical perspective of education that emphasizes promoting social transformation. Finally, I examine and defined the theory of participatory democracy, citizen democracy, which is often associated with progressive communitarian thinking and a view of education as providing greater community partnerships. This view advocates an approach to service learning that promotes civic responsibility, but often is not clear about the nature of the higher education community partnership nor the civic outcome of service learning. I attempt to clarify some of these issues and defend this viewpoint.

NOTES

1. Jacoby and associates (1996) include cocurricular community service as service learning, provided that a reflective component is included as part of the service experience. I focus mainly on the curricular integration of service learning throughout this book, although aspects of what I have to say have application to cocurricular service.

2. Much of this research is cited in Jacoby and associates (1996).

4

Service Learning as Volunteerism and the Neoconservative Theory of Civic Literacy

As I stated previously, many adherents of service learning support this movement because they are primarily interested in the "ethic of service," or the "spirit of volunteerism." Volunteerism has a place in any good service-learning program. Students performing direct service at community-based organizations is probably the most age appropriate form of service for high school age students and college freshman. However, when the ethic of service or the spirit of volunteerism is appropriated to serve the weak democratic purpose of character formation, this has certain ramifications for educational pedagogy, the faculty role, and forms of social analysis.

THE WEAK DEMOCRACY THEORY OF THE VOLUNTEER APPROACH TO SERVICE LEARNING

Weak democracy, as I have defined it, is an approach to democracy that, while paying lip service to the importance of upholding democracy through education and other aspects of our society, advocates other values as more important. To be sure it is believed that these other values complement democracy, but often this is not articulated. The weak democracy approach that I focus on here is the neoconservative view. In the next chapter I shall consider the technocratic view.

It may strike the reader as outrageous to construe social neoconservatism as advocating "weak" democracy. Certainly prominent exponents of this outlook, such as New Gingrich, would seem, for many, to epitomize "true patriotism." At the outset one needs to draw a sharp distinction between chauvinistic forms of patriotism, versus patriotism or loyalty to the ideals upon which our country was founded. Neoconservatism certainly embodies patriotism. But to what end? The end is to America, not the values underlying America. It also adheres to a very selected interpretation of the American experience. And what is this interpretation?

The neoconservative interpretation of the American experience is one that upholds not merely the market economy, but the values of corporate America. It believes in the myth of the invisible hand of capitalism that all things will best be served by supporting opportunities for corporate capitalism to prosper. As part of this interpretation, it is believed that by providing incentives for corporations to thrive through federal and state tax deductions and reduction in the percentage of taxes paid on capital gains and other tax benefits, we all will be better off.

Defenders of this interpretation seem to overlook the impact of outsizing, the subcontracting of manufacturing of more labor intensive parts to factories in the Third World or to companies that are not unionized; and of technological displacements, such as people losing their jobs due to computerization. The net effect of these activities has been to create historically an unprecedented labor force that, which is at the time of this writing officially considered to be at a record low of unemployment. At the same time our country is experiencing a record gap between the haves and have-nots.

The management structure has been flattened, and, in the words of Rifkin (1995) companies have moved to just-in-time employment. This is a form of work that generally dispenses with middle management in favor of investing more decision making authority in the shop floor employees. Often this is done with the rationalization that employees are given more democratic power within the company, but this is misleading. In reality companies are trying to cut down on overhead by eliminating middle management and to take advantage of greater computerization to eliminate paperwork and improve the operation of the factory. If middle management is downsized, someone has to make front-line decisions. Therefore, it makes a great deal of sense from the company perspective to invest greater decisional power in work teams. Unfortunately, few salary increases accompany the increase in decision making that shop floor employees have.

The unchallenged assumptions of the neoconservative interpretation of the political economy is that there should be less rather than more government, that governmental control, whether through environmental restrictions or through insisting on adequate medical coverage for employees is economically counter productive. This viewpoint results in criticisms of the welfare system as fostering increased dependency upon the government and fails to acknowledge the extent of corporate welfare. A glaring example of this, of course, occurs when a state provides tax incentives for a major company to locate there. A number of years ago the state of Colorado tried to attract United Air Lines to relocate a larger share of its corporate activities in Denver through tax incentives which many felt would undermine the state governmental infrastructure.

In the area of values, the neoconservative approach emphasizes the importance of personal freedom in the guise of an unrestricted market economy and a decrease in personal taxes. In something of a contradiction, however, neoconservatives think nothing of wanting to use the power of the government to impose certain ethical and social values upon others, such as greater media censorship and the abolition of abortion. While being quick to ask the government to come to the aid of cooperate America to improve the economic environment, this viewpoint is also quick to blame people in poverty for being the cause of their poverty. In the climate of welfare reform, many neoconservatives advocate that forcing people to work at any job, no matter how alienating and dead end, is better than other approaches, such as providing job training and opportunities for people to gain self-sufficiency.

This view leads to a profoundly weak theory of democracy as it advocates the privatization of almost everything, including the public schools. There is an almost intentionally myopic unwillingness to acknowledge the importance of having a public. Many exponents of public schooling maintain that one of the most important functions of public school is to help create a public (Postman, 1995). Some writers (Bellah et al., 1985; Pratte, 1988a) have linked the neoconservative approach to weak democracy or to procedural republicanism, the social contractarian views of society. I suppose that many neoconservatives would support this interpretation of the sources of democracy. Indeed, there is a social conservative variation of procedural republicanism which is epitomized by the thinking of Nozick (1974). I defer a more thorough discussion of procedural republicanism until I get to the social liberal view. However, a few clarifying comments are appropriate at this point.

Procedural republicanism or weak democracy, as previously stated, is substantially derived from the social contractrarian theory of government. According to this view, government is justified by a presumed tacit agreement of people to forgo or defer the pursuit of purely private ends in favor of the benefits that accrue from agreeing to form a democracy. It is, of course, believed that the private sacrifices made in the service of democracy are more than rewarded by the protection achieved through the establishment of government that protects the weakest in society from the strongest and which provides maximal equality of opportunity.

In addition to the social contract, procedural republicanism assumes the notion of atomistic individualism, the idea that individuals are primarily self-sufficient, that we are ultimately the meaning and value giver to our lives. We "intentionally" agree to impose limits on certain self-derived ideas in the name of the social contract. But the social contract is not the source of values; it is simply the socially constructed device to ensure maximal equality of opportunity in a society composed of individuals who essentially or fundamentally want to pursue their own self-interests.

Why is a procedural republic or social contractrarian theory of democracy on the one hand, linked to a politically liberal view, advocating the importance of promoting freedom of inquiry or working for social justice (Rawls, 1971), while on the other hand, linked to social convservative and libertarian thinkers, such as Nozick, who celebrate the market economy and the value of property above all? Clearly the procedural republican view of government is not the only source for the neoconservative viewpoint.

Part of what fuels this viewpoint is not merely the privileging of individualism at the expense of the commitment to society, but the privileging of economic values. As Postman (1995) has pointed out, there are many "gods" that claim our allegiance. Underlying the neoconservative approach is not merely philosophical liberalism, but the other god of economic wealth, reinforced by materialist and consumerist mentality.

It is difficult to get a critical handle on the problems here, because procedural republicanism aggravates the problems. It does so because the concept of the atomistic individual, characteristic of procedural republicanism, prevails in this perspective. But we must recognize that merely advocating the priority of the individual does not lead to neoconservative values. The existentialist movement epitomized by Jean-Paul Sartre, who was a Marxist, provides clear evidence that there can be a philosophical defense of the privatization of human experience that does not lead to neoconservative values. Clearly there is more underlying neoconservativism than a tendency to the rationalization of the atomistic individual. Again, it is the god of economic value, the notion that what gives individuals meaning is not really faith or love, even love of country, but material acquisition. The other values, such as love of country, and faith in God serve as rationalizations of the neoconservative value of greed that undergirds this approach.

One can see that procedural republicanism reinforces the market economy outlook of neoconservatism. It does this in at least two ways. First, this view regards individuals as primarily self-interested individuals who support moral principles, such as liberty and fairness, on the presumption that it is in the ultimate or enlightened self-interest of individuals to do so. This is the social contract argument for morality. Daly (1994) points out that first in importance for procedural republicanism is the liberal claim of the priority of right. "This means that in a constitutional democracy, the guarantees of individual political and civil liberties take priority over any good that could be accomplished by rescinding those rights. Only the protection of a more basic human liberty can justify curtailing another" (Daly, 1994, p. xvi). Then, the desire for material accumulation or wealth is considered one of our fundamental rights. The only basis for criticism of such a right from the point of view of procedural republicanism would be to claim that in some sense materialism undermines the social contract or impedes a greater liberty. But because procedural republicanism generally endorses property as almost a sacred right, it becomes difficult to argue, in terms of the assumptions of procedural republicanism, that materialism and an unrestrained market economy could undermine the social contract or a greater liberty.

The other link of procedural republicanism to the support of corporate capitalism resides in the utilitarian nature of the procedural republic. This viewpoint tends to argue that the market economy is but an extension of the procedural republic. It is believed to be the form of economy that mirrors the social contract and enables individualism to thrive. Thus, procedural republicanism appears to entail limiting government because it is assumed that government control is some kind of an artificial limiting factor that is at odds with the notion of the atomistic individual and the social contract. Just as procedural republicanism subscribes to the belief that we all benefit ultimately by yoking ourselves to the social contract, so we individually and collectively will thrive by allowing individuals to pursue the making of money with the fewest restraints possible.

SERVICE AND EDUCATIONAL PEDAGOGY

The extreme deployment of the service perspective in relation to the academic integration of service is to have service as just a class option with no connection to the curriculum. Of course, by definition, this becomes mere service and not service learning. This possible use of service also can be seen on college campus with strong cocurricular service programs. Volunteerism or charity is the typical model of service in this context. Students are encouraged to adopt the spirit of volunteerism. However, other models of service, such as justice, strengthening the civic infrastructure, and contributing to community improvement, are generally not acknowledged nor valued.

Before turning to the academic implications of the volunteerist approach to service learning, I would like to register a concern about the broader ramification of this model for society at large. Encouraged by President Bill Clinton and former General Colin Powell, we have witnessed a national gathering on promoting an ethic of service in America. Community service is a popular idea, it goes without saying. But we must have concern with our society's tendency to address our societal problems with band-aid approaches. Clearly, there are natural and manmade disasters that call for massive volunteer efforts. Moreover, we need many nonprofit agencies to provide a variety of vital human services, and these organizations can not operate without volunteer support. However, we must refrain from the tendency to be content with band-aid approaches. In many cases, we need to address the underlying causes of our many social problems. If we are not careful, we may find ourselves being content with dealing with the effects of our problems rather than the causes. As Terry Pickeral says, "We need to pull people out of the stream, but we also need people to go upstream to find out why people are in the water in the first place."[1]

I am particularly concerned by a proposal of Rifkin (1995) who has recommended that rather than challenging the political economy of capitalistic technological displacement, we should recognize the value of the non-profit sector, the "third-sector," as he calls it. He suggests that we provide work for people in the third sector by providing "service vouchers" through corporate taxation. I fear we may be tempted to replace "welfare" with "service-fare," with all the attendant problems of people feeling they are given "make work." This proposal alarmingly and perhaps unintentionally could divert the service-learning movement into a direction that undermines its civic development potential, just at a time when we need to be strengthening the ways in which service learning can help mount challenges to the drift of our political economy in ways that make work redundant. I am not saying that we should move away from increased automation, but I am suggesting that we need to think about ways in which work can become democratized even in an increasingly technological society. I discuss the democratization of work in Chapter 7 as part of the effort to build sustainable democratic communities.

THE FACULTY ROLE

In one sense, it is even difficult to understand why faculty would support service learning from this perspective. If they support it, it is because they support volunteerism as a way to promote a sense of civic responsibility. However, faculty or service-learning directors seldom clarify or explain this latter concept. Faculty often resist integrating service into their courses precisely on these grounds. They define service in a volunteer mode and therefore see very little reason for doing service through a course. From this perspective, the curricular integration of service seems to undermine rather than enhance academic learning

So long as the situation focuses on the volunteer concept of service, faculty will resist integrating community service into the curriculum, which is very understandable. If there is no academic relevance of the service experience to the curriculum, why should a faculty member provide the opportunity for students to engage in service? If the faculty member supports service learning, this is probably because the faculty also subscribes to the value of experiential education. But even if this is the basis for faculty support of this pedagogy, learning objectives remain disconnected from the service objectives. The volunteer form of service, combined with experiential education, characterizes much of the way many faculty ultimately conceive of how service learning should be integrated into the curriculum.

As I stated above, some faculty contend that this approach to service learning also promotes civic literacy. But again civic literacy is being defined as equivalent to "possessing an ethic of service." I shall discuss the experiential education approach in the following chapter. Short of supporting the integration of service into a course because the inclusion is viewed partially as a form of experiential education, there appears little reason to integrate the aspects of service into the curriculum. The institution might as well put its energies into supporting cocurricular service where, for example, students perform service through a service related organization.

THE VOLUNTEER MODEL OF SERVICE LEARNING

What, it may be asked, is wrong with this conception of service learning, other than the fact that it is an approach that is disconnected from the learning objectives of the classroom? Actually, there has been considerable criticism leveled at this view within the service-learning movement, but the criticism is usually disregarded, because it is assumed that the critics are advocates of a social justice perspective, and this point of view is widely rejected or disregarded.

What sorts of criticisms are made against such an apparently benign approach to service? To begin with, this approach to service tends to limit the parameters of service simply to providing direct forms of service to the community, without assisting students in obtaining an understanding of some of the root causes of the problems. To return to the example of students working at a homeless shelter, some students will come to a deeper understanding of the causes of poverty through conversation with people living in the homeless shelter. For example, a student might suppose that all homeless people are mentally ill, drug addicts, or alcoholics. But then the student meets a young man, perhaps not much older than the student, and through conversation, the student discovers that the young man has a wife and children who are at another homeless shelter. He became homeless as a result of his carpentry tools being stolen. He took a job working at a McDonald's but was not earning enough to pay his rent, and he and his wife and child ended up on the streets.

Through such a conversation, the student may indeed to change his or her opinion regarding the causes of homelessness. But more often, students working at the homeless shelter may not have much conversation with the homeless individuals they serve, or they may talk to people who fit their stereotypes and walk away from this experience believing that the cause of homelessness is emotional and mental instability associated with drug and alcohol abuse. Unless there is guided reflection on the service experience, there is little chance that these students will have their stereotypes challenged. Perhaps if a professor has these students in a classroom in a discussion with the other student who had the conversation with the father who could not afford his rent, chances are that the other two students might end up reconsidering their position.

So we conclude that faculty-guided reflection is a good thing. However, if the faculty supports service learning out of a desire to promote an ethic of service, the faculty member has little reason to provide classroom time for such reflection. This professor would better serve his or her interests simply by having the students keep a journal about their service experiences. The journal can serve as a record of the students' service experiences and chronicle their personal, moral, and social growth if they come about. But there is certainly no reason, from the perspective of promoting an ethic of service, for relating service to the course objectives. This is why, I believe, so many professors find incorporating guided reflection on service experiences to be difficult. They essentially see no academic relevance to the service experience. And they are right, at least from the perspective of volunteerism. If all one is interested in is promoting an "ethic of service," there is nothing of particular relevance of that purpose or outcome to the course content

In one sense, the volunteer approach to service, when embedded in this way within the curriculum, seems to me to be counterproductive to both good teaching and learning and to the spirit of service itself. It is counterproductive to good teaching because students are asked to perform community service experiences unrelated to course content. This constitutes a hidden curriculum of reinforcing the notion that our social world is more random than it is. As an example of this attitude, take the phrase "Shit happens." What is more objectionable about this phrase than its scatological tone is the notion that we have very little control over social events. This attitude is reflective of cynicism and leads to the "Generation X" phenomenon, if there is one, of opting out from assuming responsibility for what is occurring in the world around us.

Although the voluntary viewpoint is animated by a spirit of "giving back to the community," by refusing to use academic resources in the spirit of trying to contribute to the improvement of community life, this approach actually can have the effect of making things worse. It makes things worse by reinforcing elitist patronizing attitudes toward the poor. It leaves the community even more guarded about young people coming in and doing things to them, rather than entering the community in a spirit of collaboration. Worst of all, perhaps, the spirit of volunteerism expressed in this way reinforces the elitist values of noblesse oblige, that the wealthy deserve their affluence so long as they share their largesse with the have-nots. This attitude historically has even been assumed at times by people in poverty as they acquiesce to their own conditions of servitude. Of course, from the neoconservative perspective, there is nothing wrong with all of this. The neoconservative believes that people are to blame essentially for their poverty, that the wealthy deserve their wealth because they have attained this through individual effort. This is an agenda of volunteerism that is in line with the neoconservative philosophy.

THE NEOCONSERVATIVE VIEW OF CIVIC LITERACY

What then is the view of civic literacy or civic education implicit in the neoconservative approach? In practical terms, the view of civic literacy is one that advocates citizen involvement in securing the least amount of government possible, at least in so far as when government is directed toward the redistribution of wealth. It supports the government in strengthening corporate capitalism and in upholding its views of morality, such as banning abortion, limiting the rights of homosexuals, and punishing those who are too critical of our society, to name just a few neoconservative values.

The volunteer view of civic literacy, is, as I said, one of weak democracy. It pays nominal lip service to the values of democracy, but mainly gives allegiance to America, the country. At its extreme, neoconservatives do not want students to develop critical thinking skills, at least in terms of examining the foundations of democratic capitalism. Students should have had their values inculcated by church and family by the time they are of college age, and their main responsibility is to be good hardworking Americans, supporting the litany of neoconservative values that reinforces corporate capitalism and paternalism. Probed to the bone, this outlook really does not care about civic life, about a sense of the public. It prefers a more trivial society of religious and class-stratified enclaves, typified by gated communities. But, of course, in its extreme versions, this point of view is not above wanting to allow its own values to be imposed upon others in the name of God. Fundamentalism is, of course, a major source of this kind of neoconservative outlook. But I do not see "religious faith" as the source of this neoconservative outlook, only as another ideology that reinforces its privatistic, corporate capitalistic outlook. The neoconservative socialization view of civic education is virtually equivalent to the moral character education philosophy (Wynne, 1987/88).[2] Writers of this ilk believe that the most important role of education in relation to moral and civic development is instilling moral virtues and a sense patriotism. According to Wynne, "Adults should set the key policies and rules, and the young should respectfully obey and learn" (1991, p. 153). This often is considered an indoctrinative view of moral or civic education in the sense that young people are taught to accept certain values regardless of the evidence or justification for them.

I doubt that anyone would disagree about the value of some degree of direct moral instruction for young children. However, this approach becomes problematic as an approach to civic education. Democratic understanding requires that its participants value not only a commitment to decisions enacted for the common good but that they arrive at these decisions independently and rationally. As Briand (In press) says, it is insufficient simply to tell children what the "correct" views are. Children need to become practiced in the procedure of democratic decision making.

One might challenge this view by suggesting that young children are insufficiently mature to make this effort. To this I would only ask the reader to reflect on his or her own early childhood experiences of fairness. Do we not have an elementary concept of fair treatment even as young children? Children may at times be unruly and difficult to deal with; that is, their "moral character" may be in the process of formation. But as important as helping children directly understand right from wrong, we must allow children to develop their ability to participate in the democratic process.

The social conservative view, when applied to older students tends to uphold what Giroux (1983) calls the "citizenship transmission" view. The basic idea holds that young people should be inculcated in the basic information about how the government works and at the same time should be encouraged to remain patriotic. This view, of course, extends beyond the social conservative camp. A related problem with the civic education as socialization view is that it is promoted by an outlook that has an inherent tension regarding the nature and the role of individualism. On the one hand, this conservative outlook tends to stress the importance of rights and responsibilities of the individual against the attempts of the state, through the democratic process, to impose limits on individual initiative, especially as it pertains to business and the market economy. But at the same time, the socialization view fails to appreciate fully that the kind of autonomy advocated for adults would have little likelihood of developing in the young if its indoctrinative view of moral and civic education were completely successful. This is the case because this view attempts to get young people to adopt basic ethical beliefs on the basis of authority and regardless of the evidence. This view of civic literacy combines an authoritarian view of morality and civic education with a libertarian view of the market economy. This highlights the inherent contradiction in the conservative view that young people have little sense or ability to engage in independent thinking. Democracy is paid lip service but is not practiced. This outlook is unable to achieve the truly democratic results that are desired.

The social conservative agenda is motivated either by a desire to remove governmental restrictions, such as in advocating the privatization of education, or by a desire to assure that people conform to their ideology. The neoconservative opposition to abortion is intelligible in this light. Organizations, such as Operation Rescue may proclaim they are concerned about the "rights" of the unborn. But abortion opponents in this movement uphold of the patriarchal family in which women are subordinate to men. Upholding the "traditional family" is important for neoconservatives because it assumes this kind of family will foster the civically dependent individual essential to the neoconservative perspective.

The ethic of service, or volunteer approach becomes a logical choice for neoconservativism. The conservative concept of civic responsibility, which is alleged to follow from volunteerism, is vague to say the least. In reality, students are taught the hidden curriculum of privatization, of seeing everything in individualistic terms, of seeing the world in random terms, in not having to assume any social responsibility for why the social world is the way it is.

THE TRADITIONALIST VIEW OF EDUCATION

Before proceeding further, I would like briefly to contrast the neo-conservative approach to civic literacy with another variation of weak democracy, the academic traditionalist approach that emphasizes autonomy or freedom. It is precisely the lack of a focus on property rights that seems to create the difference between the traditionalist approach and neoconservative approach. As we have seen, the neoconservative approach emphasizes a minimal role of government out of a desire to protect the economic freedom or autonomy of the individual. The neoconservatives have a double standard of advocating individual freedom but at the same time want to impose limits on the freedom of others who do not share their views on the right to life or prayer in the schools. This double standard is understandable from the perspective of the neoconservative foundational value of economic freedom. The rights of individuals are important insofar as they contribute to the maximization of the economic freedom of the individual.

The academic traditionalist or academic fundamentalist has a different concept of liberty. The traditionalist places the greatest value on personal, spiritual, and intellectual liberty of the individual, instead of on economic freedom. The academic traditionalist favors education as the primary means by which these individualist values can be achieved. This viewpoint epitomizes the great tradition approach within higher education. According to the great tradition, the lasting contribution of a university education is to provide students with the knowledge and intellectual tools to continue their growth in knowledge and understanding as informed by the traditions of the liberal arts and sciences. In terms of this viewpoint a form of universal education promotes lasting social progress.

Because academic traditionalists focus on education for its own sake, they see little value in service learning. In fact traditionalists view service learning is a form of applied learning that dilutes the traditional curriculum. Civic literacy is viewed, like the viewpoint of instrumental reason, as mainly consisting of being knowledgeable and being a responsible voter. And like the instrumentalist approach, those attracted to the traditionalist perspective, are leery of more populist forms of government, fearing that uneducated decisions may result.

The traditionalist approach places an inordinate faith in moral education of the young. Whereas the neoconservatives want to achieve a kind of indoctrination of the young, the traditionalist is clearly an advocate of critical thinking. Traditionalists place an unqualified faith in the power of the educated autonomous individual to make the right choices. This viewpoint has typically been criticized by neo-Marxists as failing to understand how individuals are not completely autonomous. They argue that individuals are subject to educational approaches that have a hidden curriculum of conditioning students to serve the interests of corporate capitalism under the guise of the great tradition. In fact, according to neo-Marxist critics, the great tradition itself constitutes part of the hegemony that makes it difficult for students to understand the ways in which traditionalist education serves as a mechanism to reinforce class division. The great tradition does so, it is alleged, by creating the illusion that choices are primarily a product of individual character, rather than partly being a product of the social circumstances in which we are stipulated.

The traditionalist approach flounders on its ambivalence to the relationship of education to society. Believing, as it does, that education in the traditionalist spirit is the primary vehicle for achieving the good society, this approach adopts a suspicious and critical eye toward more overt attempts to create a more just society. It is believed that rather than improving society, more praxis-oriented approaches will only succeed in diluting the educational process and leaving people without the necessary educational resources to improve society.

I shall not further critique traditionalist approach. I refer the reader instead to the writings of people such as Henry Giroux and Ira Schor (1986). I, of course, have little sympathy with the traditionalist approach. And I certainly agree with radical critiques of this approach that it fails to understand the co-optive nature of education and misrepresents the nature and extent of individual autonomy as a factor in working for and achieving the good society. I discuss academic fundamentalism in the final chapter as part of a brief survey of how higher education has arrived at its position in relation to issues of social responsibility.

NOTES

1. Personal conversation.

2. All individuals go through a socialization process in which we internalize the social values of our society. The neoconservatives want to be more intentional in the socialization process that includes indoctrination (defined above) as well as a view that puts full weight on "instilling" values in children to the exclusion of critical inquiry.

5

Service Learning as Experiential Education and Consumerist Politics

The theory that I examine in this chapter is less loosely grounded in a version of weak democracy than the other views I take up. Nevertheless, this view is important because the overall perspective characterizes so much social thinking within education today.

THE CONSUMERIST THEORY OF WEAK DEMOCRACY

Briand (In press) discusses as one example of what he calls "impractical politics" the view of politics associated with the status quo, the consumerist approach to politics. Rimmerman (1997a) calls this brand of politics, elitist politics. This kind of politics concentrates on getting to solutions quickly and supports a belief that leaders are the ones who can provide the best solutions to our problems. This type of politics devotes considerable time to assessing people's needs. Briand points out that the consumerist interpretation of democratic politics regards the public as little more than a loose collection of individuals and groups, each with their own opinions, interests, and positions that must be reconciled in a way that does not unfairly disadvantage anyone. Coming close to satisfying every individual's and group's desires achieves the best result (p. 18). In effect, this version of politics transfers political decision making from the public, where it belongs, "to the policy making arena—to government hearings, school board meetings, sessions of city councils and state and national legislatures, and (sometimes) even courtrooms"(p. 19). According to Rimmerman (1997a), the public is regarded as mainly a source of accountability. Vested interest

groups, and particularly those with a lot of money exercise a disproportionate amount of influence on the outcome of these deliberations. Rimmerman
states, "The language associated with conventional politics is rooted in
'advocacy and winning'" (p. 24).

Briand claims that four major shortcomings in this brand of politics, and
each show symptoms of our inability to deliberate together as a public. First,
this process creates results that many consider to be morally unacceptable.
Cities that continue to allow virtually unlimited real estate expansion to the
detriment of the environment constitute one of countless examples. Second,
this kind of politics frequently creates political gridlock. We recall the 1995
budget showdown between the Republicans and President Clinton, which
threatened to shut the government down for a lengthy period of time as an
example of this. Third, the net effect of this decision making process
promotes coercive responses. People engage in "blocking action." This is
associated with NIMBY ("not in my back yard") politics. Briand notes that
almost every effort to build prisons, highways, power plants, mental health
facilities, and low-income housing is blocked by people who live in the
community where the new construction or facilities are planned (p. 24). A
recent example of this in Colorado was the failure of a tax referendum to
support the expansion of desperately needed light rail. Despite the fact that
the Denver area faces serious traffic gridlock in the very near future, a
majority of the citizens refused to support light rail expansion.

Finally, consumerist politics "undermines the taking of personal
responsibility for the difficult decisions that inevitably arise in public life"
(Briand, p. 19). Welfare reform, in my opinion, is a good example of this.
Rather than trying to come together in local communities to wrestle with the
many complexities of this problem, our society allows the federal government to impose a vastly overly simplistic "solution" to the problem that will
likely wreck havoc in the lives of hundreds of thousands of people once the
five-year lifetime umbrella of welfare coverage runs out for individuals. This
policy also may lead to increased crime, hopelessness, and neighborhood
deterioration across the country.

Weak democracy or procedural republicanism reinforces the consumerist
view of politics, if it is not caused by this approach. Procedural republicanism encourages the kind of market economy we have, again believing that
the least amount of government control of the economy possible ensures the
maximization of individual and economic freedom and will, it is assumed,
lead to the best alternative we have under democracy for a good society.
Unfortunately, with limited governmental controls and few limitations on the
entrepreneurial market economy, it should not be surprising that not only
are we overwhelmed by "consumerist values" through the media but that

this approach has led, not to the maximization of social justice, but to the disproportionate concentration of wealth among the economic elite in our society. The economic elite, individually and through the exercise of corporate power, supports strong interest groups that, in turn, exercise a disproportionate influence on who gets elected locally, state-wide, and nationally and what legislation gets passed.

As citizens find that their voices are ignored in the democratic representational process, individuals become discouraged. They react with apathy, and in many cases with a negative attitude, not supporting any legislation, even when their interests are served. As I have previously mentioned, the Reagan/Bush era succeeded in pitting the middle class against the lower class and created the impression that the problem with society was too much government. The public knows that the problem is not just government itself. We are aware that corporate America exercises a disproportionate share of political clout, unduly influencing legislators. But the zero-sum mentality of the procedural republican approach (because of its derivation from the concept of government being sustained through support of subordinating immediate self-interests to enlightened self-interests) encourages the public to think that consumerist politics is the only game in town as opposed to considering the option of strengthening participatory democracy. Consequently, people end up criticizing government itself instead of the political economic system that corrupts and undermines representative democracy.

The above mentioned obstacles to a more vital civic participation tend to create a lack of political efficacy and even a lack of civic obligation itself among ordinary citizens. Voter apathy reflects this. These problems are reinforced by an elitist process of legal and administrative barriers to voting, such as complicated voter registration forms (Rimmerman, 1997a). These barriers impede the affluent and well-educated more than the poor and the undereducated (Rimmerman, 1997a, p. 35). Rimmerman states that the attributes most likely to be associated with a willingness on the part of individuals to vote, from education to positive feelings about politics, are more likely to be present among the more affluent (1997a, p. 36).

If civic indifference characterizes ordinary citizens, it also manifests itself among college students. The 1992–1993 Kettering Foundation Harwood Group study of college students' views of politics concluded that students saw little value in voting and signing petitions, or in joining interest groups or in protesting (Rimmerman, 1997a, p. 43). The study also found that students contend that they are not learning to practice politics at college. Rimmerman observes, "This study revealed that many students were alienated from politics and not particularly hopeful about the future" (p. 44).

EDUCATION AND CONSUMERIST POLITICS

One of the disillusioning flash points of reality in the 1960s, as a result of the Vietnam War, was the realization that education itself, contrary to the liberal expectation that it could liberate us from injustice and continuously improve society, was susceptible to influence by consumerist politics. This realization, of course, led to massive protests during the Vietnam War, especially among college students who berated the military, industrial, and educational complex. I remember the sad time when the mathematics building at the University of Wisconsin–Madison was destroyed by a student protestor because of the belief that the mathematics department had sold out to the military by engaging in military related research.

I want to leave aside discussion of the issue of overt educational support for consumerist politics since I shall take this up in the final chapter. Instead, what I wish to discuss here is the affinity for or interrelationship between the dominant contemporary educational paradigms and consumerist politics. The dominant paradigms are scientism and instrumental reason. The corporate capitalistic substructure and consumerist politics reinforce these values in many ways because this superstructure is upheld to a great extent by this educational paradigm. And because these paradigms have a great impact on our approach to politics and service learning, I want to take up each aspect of this paradigm.

Scientism

For many reasons, scientific theory has enjoyed a prominence over other forms of intellectual theory. Scientific achievement itself is one of these reasons. I doubt that many would dispute this deserved theoretical prominence. But occupying a theoretically privileged position does not mean or entail that other important forms of theory within intellectual discourse have no place. Privileging science at the expense of recognizing and valuing other intellectual forms of human and social analysis propagates *scientism*. This view holds that science is the preferred, if not the only, foundation of knowledge and understanding of our human and social condition. Appropriate to the topic of service learning, ethical theory is illustrative of the problem we have confronted historically.

During the last two-thirds of our century there have been attempts within English and American philosophy to assimilate ethics to science, or the very opposite tendency of dismissing ethical claims as mere subjective prefer-ences. The quasi-scientific version of ethics has been known as ethical naturalism, the view that ethical values are in some sense qualities of human nature. For example, in one popular view, to say that an act is right is to say that it is one that promotes pleasure or satisfies desires. This view has been criticized for committing the "naturalistic fallacy," which essentially means equating the "desirable" with the "desired," which are, in fact different concepts. Dewey even attempted at one point in his career, to develop a "scientific" theory of values (1939) and a "science of human nature" (1922/1957). Unfortunately, Dewey never quite worked out an adequate theory of ethics (Lisman, In press). The view at the other extreme, ethical subjectivism, has been critiqued mainly for failing to recognize that ethical decision making and action is far more complex than representing a decision of personal preference or emotional approval or disapproval. In fact, a case can be made that the concepts of approval and disapproval presuppose moral concepts rather than the converse (Solomon, 1983).

These changing positions on ethics illustrate the unease we feel with regard to nonscientific forms of theorizing as applied to human beings and our society. It is as if we feel that if something can not be established on scientific grounds, then it has no validity at all.

The Dominance of Instrumental Reason

Another aspect of this phenomenon has been the tendency to replace normative issues concerning social purposes with technocratic proposals. According to Habermas (1974), it is difficult from this vantage point to distinguish between practical and technical power. This has resulted in the reduction of theory or rationality to a process of seeking sociotechnical control rather than in an attempt to create an existentially and socially meaningful understanding of the purposes of human life. A tendency exists to dismiss humanities informed approaches that discuss the importance of interrogating the good life (Taylor, 1989), or of seeking a deepening understanding of the purposes of human life. Another way of saying this is that we have a tendency to replace more subtle and complicated forms of moral and social investigation with instrumental reason (Taylor, 1991). Instrumental reason is rampant in our approach to understanding our society. For example, this perspective occurs in discussions of the economy. Economists discuss cycles of inflation and recession, creating the impression that our society and others are held captive to a kind of economic determinism that we can do little about.

Scientism and instrumental reason play into the hand of consumerist politics, thus creating the impression that only "experts" can solve our many problems. Citizens are discouraged from coming together in their local communities and addressing their immediate concerns about the deterioration of the environment, suburban sprawl, crime, congested highways, inadequate child care, and lack of individual economic opportunities. Local and state legislators and the local university tell them that the problems are too large for them handle. Experts are needed. Not surprisingly, when experts show up to testify before city councils and state legislative committees, all too often these experts are hired by vested corporate interest groups.

This kind of politics discourages citizen discussion about whether the economy should be structured in the way it is and whether social and political efforts should be mounted through the democratic process to improve society. Not only is this technocratic outlook seriously questionable, but it tends to discourage efforts to challenge the existing economic hegemony. It fuels a sense of fatalism and undermines efforts at economic transformation aimed at reducing the growing gap between the haves and have nots in our society.

Instrumental reason also creates a momentum of providing national priorities that are amenable to scientific and technocratic manipulation. Hence, much effort is spent on addressing concerns such as health problems, improving farming techniques, and developing ever more sophisticated objects of consumption. But most of us realize that improved farming techniques or even medical advances can only take us so far. As I stated in the first chapter, we must confront the question of how we deal with economic inequality, urban sprawl, misuse of our land and water resources, limited medical resources, and, especially, their limited availability to impoverished families and individuals. And of course we must cope with the negative effects of excessive materialism. These problems can be solved through technological advances alone; they require much social debate and prioritizing through the democratic processes concerning our vision of the good life and the good society and ways that we may realize this vision. Surely, technology can be a great asset to the achievement of our vision. But it can not replace a more spiritually and humanely informed vision.

Unfortunately, technocratic dominance tends to undermine the attempt civically to reclaim our social priorities. We are inclined to seek the opinion of experts as we engage in civic deliberation. Too often the very experts that we seek frame the problems in ways that are not amenable to civic solutions but tend to be self-serving instrumentalist solutions. Our civic efforts also are often impeded by an accompanying social and political perspectives that promotes an ethos of individualism and a non-systemic understanding of social and economic forces. Our scientific and technological biases overpower normative forms of individual and social understanding.

Although a subject for another essay, it should be noted that much postmodernist analysis, such as Rorty (1979), although offered in the spirit of deconstructing instrumental reason, scientism, and other ideologies, cumulatively seems to have the opposite effect of reinforcing relativism, an implication which Rorty disavows (Rorty, 1989/1997). It does so through advocating the abolition of any "foundational" epistemological (theory of knowledge) and ethical approaches. Ironically, the upshot of Rorty's work has been a revival of epistemological and ethical pragmatism, the view that we decide what is true, good, and right on the basis of what "works," itself another variant on instrumentalist reason. Even Barber (1984), who is otherwise an advocate of a more civically engaged philosophy of education, succumbs to this kind of postmodernist thinking.

IMPLICATIONS OF SCIENTISM AND INSTRUMENTALIST REASON IN THE SERVICE OF CONSUMERIST POLITICS

This complex has serious implications for pedagogy, the faculty role in education, service learning, and social analysis. I shall briefly discuss these implications. (These implications are illustrated in Table One.)

Pedagogy

First, in terms of pedagogy, our educational institutions often favor a scientific-based curriculum, valuing quantitative research over more qualitative research. They often regard humanities-based programs as the poor step-child. Jobs in scientific-related fields command higher wages than the humanities which reinforces this kind of intellectual stratification.

Second, instrumental reason is privileged in a variety of ways. In the first place, education for work is emphasized over education for democracy. The federal school-to-work initiative in which many states are developing grades K–16 partnerships to promote career awareness, especially in technical areas is a recent example of the privileging of education for work over education for democracy. Because the school-to-work initiative emphasizes work-based learning, a form of experiential education, this initiative has created some tension and confusion for the service-learning movement, obviously another form of experiential education, but having a civic, instead of a vocational, outcome. I discuss the school-to-work initiative further toward the end of this chapter.

Certainly, any institution of higher education would fail if it did not prepare its students for the workforce. But, as many policy thinkers are beginning to understand, students should be instilled with the capacity not only to be a productive member of the workforce but of the polis as well. In effect, we need to produce greater social capital, as Putnam claims (1995a,

1995b). We can not take our workforce and economic structure as a given, as Rifkin (1995) has recently warned us. We must be prepared to examine our economic priorities in light of increased technological development, and we must educate our students to be able thoughtfully to examine our economic and civic purposes.

Rifkin (1995) and Putnam (1993, 1995a, 1995b) maintain that the development of a strong civic infrastructure, or social capital, is essential to economic sustainability. Unfortunately, rather than working to create forms of education that achieve this need of greater critical scrutiny of our social goals, instrumental reason holds sway. It does so not only through scientism, the privileging of science at the expense of the humanities, but in advocating standardized forms of teaching and learning, such as certain forms of competency-based education with "teacher-proof" (Apple, 1989) prescribed objectives intended to assure that students fit into the political and economic structure in a fundamentally unquestioning way. Ironically, "critical thinking" is often one of the prescribed outcomes. But if critical thinking is taught in a prescribed, formalistic way, true critical thinking, in the sense of developing refined and subtle abilities to examine fundamental individual and social values, is undermined.

Another example of the privileging of instrumental reason is the increasing effort to expand distance-learning and computer-based instruction, thereby reducing the role of the faculty in facilitating learning. Concerns about job protection fuel faculty resistance to these technologies. A fear of being replaced by a computer; and, admittedly, the replacement of intellectual work by a computer can be not only unnerving but destructive of our sense of self-esteem. We recently witnessed this impact on Gary Kasparov in his chess match with IBM's Deep Blue supercomputer.

This technological trend constitutes a challenge and an opportunity to faculty and education generally. We must discover solid pedagogical reasons for retaining faculty who in some sense will be replaceable by computer-based instruction. Faculty should recognize that clinging to traditional forms of instruction will surely lead to their becoming redundant and atavistic. Perhaps if faculty begin to redefine their role in terms of critical pedagogy and civically engaged scholarship, they will not be as replaceable.

The Experiential Education Model of Service Learning

With respect to models of service learning, the tendency for some faculty to define service learning merely as experiential education may reflect the scientific bias in education. The professor may believe that in focusing on experiential education he or she may be able to avoid dealing with the "messiness" of values.

To be fair, many faculty who engage in the curricular integration of service learning do so because they see experiential learning as simply a better way for students to learn. Many faculty members focus first and foremost on their discipline, and will embrace a pedagogy if they feel it is a more effective way to teach and for students to learn. Many such faculty members adopt this form of experiential learning out of good hearted motives. In providing a critique of experiential education as it is linked to consumer politics and scientism and instrumental reason, I do not mean to claim that faculty who support service learning as an effective pedagogy necessarily are reflective of this hegemony of weak democracy. I mainly am interested in clarifying how this public philosophy can reinforce this purpose of service learning.

In passing, I might mention that instrumental reason may unwittingly influence faculty who adopt an approach to service learning that emphasizes promoting an individualistic spirit of volunteerism. This reinforces instrumental reason by feeding into an individualistic ethos, which I discuss further below, having the cumulative effect of relegating systematic planning to the information and efficiency experts. Students frequently are plugged into the existing social service and governmental agencies that set the social agenda. These who set the agenda seek assistance from the university or college to the extent that it can provide information or students to help the agencies achieve their prescribed goals.

As McKnight (1995) has repeatedly warned us, often these agencies do more harm than good to the members of the communities they serve, mainly through a deficit approach to social and community service, defining people as having problems rather than assets. So long as service learning is confined to a form of experiential education linked to involving students in acts of charity, as valuable as that is, service learning may derail attempts of higher education to serve as a mediating institution contributing to the development of a more just and democratic society.

One of the major difficulties with the experiential education model of service learning is that this approach fails to explain why experiential education should be carried out through community service. If the goal is mainly to provide students with real world experiences, the only important objective is for experiential experience to be relevant to the subject matter or the course objectives. So to take an extreme example, a business student could work in an insurance office as an intern in a management course, assisting in the company's operation. There is, of course, no connection to service in this example.

One might reply that one of the reasons for having a student volunteer in a nonprofit organization is to assure that the learning experiences are diverse. Diverse experiences enables the student to relate or correlate academic material to a variety of experiences. So, a student in a journalism course, might work on a community newspaper or for the local daily paper to attain such diverse experiences. Regardless of the diversity of experiences associated with experiential learning, this approach to service learning remains disconnected from any civic purposes of service learning. This, of course, actually departs from service learning, as we have defined it.

As I previously stated, work-based learning represents a form of experiential education. The federal school-to-work legislation defines service learning as one form of school-to-work pedagogy. Early on I mentioned that career exploration constitutes a valuable benefit of service learning. Students explore careers often in the course of doing community service. Career exploration can be done as an aspect of service learning. However, the converse does not hold. Service learning is not identical to work-based learning. Students explore careers and investigate the relevance of internships and co-op experiences in school-to-work programs. And these can be valuable programs. Young people, especially those still in high school should be able to explore technical career opportunities that do not necessarily require a college degree. Many traditionalists resist this kind of direction in applied learning. They believe students should receive a liberal arts education even if he or she ends up in a technical career. Unfortunately, many people who obtain liberal arts degree work at least for a number of years in occupations unrelated to their professions. Many parents have become impatient with paying large sums of money for their children to obtain college degrees only to see them working in low paying jobs for many years afterward. Nevertheless, as valuable as work-based learning may be, this form of learning is not identical to service learning.[1]

Forms of Social Analysis

Turning to forms of social analysis, there exists an unauthentic theoretic and an atheoretic force at play. The unauthentic mode of theory, linked to scientism, is pervasive in our institutions of higher education. This approach often produces research aimed at social control through behavioristic modes of analyses and functional sociology.[2] In one sense, welfare reform has been the victim of such analysis. A conservative critique and also simplistic forms of social analysis concludes that the poverty problem can be mini-mized by removing the work disincentives of the Aid for Families with Dependent Children program. Few would doubt that pernicious disincentives exist in the old system, but this accounts for only a fraction of the social issues of poverty. Incidentally, Dewey (1927, 1938, 1956), who is often praised by writers in the service learning movement as a proponent of experiential education and an advocate of moving away from a privatized understanding of experience and society, although exceptional in that respect, attempted to conceptualize human experience in behavioristic and scientific terms broadly conceived.

The tendency of faculty and students to uphold a shallow form of individualism in which social problems are regarded as almost exclusively the product of faulty human character represents an atheoretic force, linked to instrumental reason. This view neglects the considerable sociological literature that highlights the degree to which problems are rooted in pervasive patterns of economic and social injustice rather than in the faults of individuals. Bellah and his associates (1985) write persuasively of our resistance to think against this excessively individualistic mode. Taylor (1991) maintains that this kind of focus on individualism is self-defeating, leaving people bereft of the sense of individual self-fulfillment that was the point of their individualism. Taylor bases his solution on the recognition of our essential sociality, that we can only find individual self-fulfillment through dialogical engagement with others and our community. Sandel (1996) has chronicled the history of the development of the social contractarian understanding of society, the "procedural Republic" that has reinforced both instrumental reason and the atomistic view of the individual rampant in our society and in educational institutions. I summarize Sandel's analysis in Chapter 7.

Faculty

Mandarin professors maintain their elite positions through conspiring with a research and publication reward system that produces countless articles and books of frequently self-serving theory that are of limited use and are often only intelligible to scholars within one's own circle. The faculty reward system, which provides tenure and promotion on the basis of traditional scholarship, institutional service, and traditional teaching, fosters an atmosphere of perpetuating the worst aspects of the ivory tower syndrome. I discuss this phenomenon further in the final chapter.

This paradigm also embroils community college faculty members. Faculty often perpetuate the lecture method, emphasizing an uncritical form of pedagogy in which students are held accountable for the mastery of information rather than truly empowering critical thinking. Faculty resistance to thinking more intentionally and effectively about how they teach and persisting with a traditional form of teaching as information delivery, what Frerie (1970) calls the "banking method," reflects the fact that they may have bought into or succumbed to instrumental reason. Community college faculty seldom see their faculty role as having any relevance to the community.

Faculty resistance to thinking through the various models of service learning that challenge the status quo must be seen again as succumbing to the dominant values of society. In contrast, to use a phrase of Giroux (1988), we need teachers who are transformative intellectuals, dedicated to helping students become more effective critical thinkers and actors in the service of promoting a more democratically just society.

Table One
Consumerist Politics and Its Educational Paradigm

Consumerist Politics and Education	Pedagogy	Service Learning	Social Analysis	Faculty
Scientism	• Humanities devalued • Overvaluation of science • Subjectivity and relativity of values	• Tendency to reduce service learning to value-free experiential education	• Quantitative research • Socioligical functionalism	• Faculty ivory tower syndrome • Faculty reward system reinforces the scientific model of scholarship
Instrumental Reason	• Education for work • Competency-based education • Distance learning and computer-assisted instruction	• Ethos of individualistic volunteerism • Deficit approach to community analysis	• Privatized approach to social issues	• Traditional teaching emphasizing processing information and faculty disengagement from community

THE CONSUMERIST THEORY OF CIVIC LITERACY

In terms of this view, civic literacy is mainly understanding how the government works, and civic virtue is displayed by making trips to the voting box. Giroux (1983) calls this the "social science model" of civic literacy. Within education, this approach includes:

(1) a claim to high-status knowledge and equality with other academic disciplines based upon a firm commitment in the social sciences; (2) a claim to the "truth" based upon a view of social science knowledge as "correct" in a relatively unproblematic way; (3) support for an epistemology based on reflectionalist notions

of learning in which the mastery of specific social science knowledge and skills would offset the half-truths and mystifications inherent in "common sense" knowledge; (4) support for a hierarchical view of knowledge and a concomitant view of social relationships. (pp. 181–182)

Giroux adds that this view values as knowledge a "notion of objectivity that results in a pedagogy that celebrates inquiry, concept discovery, and various other forms of inductive thinking. What appears to be discovery learning ends up as a series of pedagogical methods in which knowledge is depoliticized and objectively 'fixed'." In the final chapter I discuss how the history of the development of institutions of higher education has reinforced this approach.

Those who defend representative democracy and a limited role for the populace represent this view of civic literacy. People of this persuasion believe that the less political involvement of the masses, the better off we are. According to Barber (1984), this view of democracy upholds that notion that the best form of government is one that places decision making in the hands of experts.

Morse (1989) provides a more neutral description of this view of democracy and the necessary civic skills. In fact, she draws a distinction between "electoral competitive democracy" and "representative democracy" (p. 62). The first version of democracy advocates that freedoms will exist if open competition is in place. It represents special interest politics among the elected, and limits the rule of citizens in making decisions about policy. Citizens should be well schooled in the process of voting, actually do it, and have knowledge of candidates' abilities and platforms. "This philosophy of politics narrows its perspective to government and the activities of elected officials. Involvement would exclude all other areas of life (schools, churches, coporations), even though decisions made in those arenas might affect the entire community" (Morse, 1989, p. 63). Morse claims for this model to work, citizens must exercise tolerance in letting different perspectives come before the electorate.

The second model, representaive democracy, goes beyond the electoral process in two ways: "Leaders must be responsible to the electorate, and certain basic freedoms are spelled out and guaranteed" (Morse, 1989, p. 62). This form of democracy spawns citizen involvement in interest groups, calls on citizens to express opinions on public policity issues, and stimulates other forms of nonelectoral political participation. "Representative democracy requires that citizens be knowledgeable on issues so they can evaluate the peformance of elected officials, support the electoral process, and be able to judge public policy decision making" (Morse, 1989, p. 63). Morse adds,

"The primary criticism of this model is that it is oriented toward special interests, does not encompass the concept of collective good, and fundamentally limits the citizen's role to participate once the vote is cast" (p. 63). For the purposes of my discussion, I consider these two forms of democracy to be two aspects of consummerist politics.

This approach to politics also typically upholds the consumerist version of the community decision-making process of local government experts in deciding what is best for a community. Of course, elected officials or city management perform this function, creating the appearance of democratically public officials representing the commonweal. But all too often decisions that affect the well being of an entire city are made with, at best, only nominal consultation with community members. This process of decision making is recreated time and again in municipality after municipality.

All too often through the influence of powerful business leaders in the community, business interests are put ahead of other interests, such as the health of the community. For example, it might be to the interests of citizens to limit growth through not allowing unwieldy real estate expansion. But members of the community never have a chance to vote on this matter. Instead, they can turn to their local television channels and watch the city mayor and council proceedings as housing developers make their proposals for continued urban sprawl.

With this viewpoint, we are, I think, at the heart of the source of much of our civic distemper. Many people feel distempered, and in fact, because of disuse or no use, they lack the civic imagination even to consider how they might play a role in making important local decisions about the well-being of the community. People do not cheerfully relinquish their citizenship role. Being denied the opportunity to participate in the civic process or decision-making process and seeing things going in directions that do not benefit them or are against their interests, these citizens become disgruntled. They are among those vocal critics of government who want to limit the role of government because they can not imagine government serving their interests. It seems obvious that the reclaiming of politics at the local level will help diminish this cynical and negative view of government and politics.

NOTES

1. Sigmond (Sigmond et al., 1996) supports the notion of work-based learning as service learning. He states, "Estimates suggest that over one-half of college students work for pay during their under-graduate years. Many workplaces speak of customer service as being a learning organization. There is increased potential for linking service and learning when students work for pay. This is a vastly under-

explored form of Service-Learning" (p. 13) In my opinion, this view of service learning is too inclusive, and if embraced by colleges and universities would undermine the social justice and citizen-building thrust of this movement.

2. According to Ballantine (1989) functionalist theory is the approach of sociology that assumes that "society and institutions within society, such as education, are made up of interdependent parts all working together, each contributing some necessary activity to the functioning of the whole society" (p. 8). Functional theorists focus their research on questions concerning the structure and functioning of organizations. The problem with this approach "is that it fails to recognize the number of divergent interests, ideologies, and conflicting interest groups in society" (p. 9).

6

Service Learning as Justice

Many people have become attracted to service learning out of a desire for education to increase its capacity to achieve a more just society. Advocates of this approach criticize the "charity" or "volunteerist" approach and even the "civic approach." In the next chapter I argue that this critique of the "civic approach" is founded on a number of misunderstandings. Suffice it to say for now, that justice advocates are impatient with any attempt to deflect service learning from achieving social transformation.

Critics argue that this approach within higher education violates the principle of liberal neutrality essential for institutions of education to achieve their purposes. Professor should ensure that contrasting opinions regarding major issues should be impartially presented. For example, contrasting views on managed health care should be presented in a public policy course. Many justice advocates use their class room for their own personal soap boxes, in fact feeling quite strongly that they have a duty to advocate on behalf of a specific cause. So in the case of health care, perhaps a justice advocate might stack the case in favor of a socialized health care program, dismissing managed care and other approaches as "ridiculous." Moreover, the social justice approach, which concerns itself with seeking social transformation, appears at the outset to set in process a confrontational approach to community work. The affluent, corporate capitalism or institutional racism are the enemies, and the marginalized, the under-represented, the economically dispossessed are the good guys.

Despite these difficulties, I am sympathetic with the justice perspective. We must use our educational resources for the improvement of civic and community life, and we must recognize that we need not merely provide service to members of our society, but we should address the root causes of our societal problems.

Mendel-Reyes (1997), representing a justice approach to service learning, states that the social justice model places a premium on the attack of root cases, head on. Mendel-Reyes writes about her pilgrimage into higher education that involved grass roots organizing for the United Farm Workers. Mendel-Reyes, although aware of the tension between what I am calling the participatory democracy view of service learning and the justice approach, clearly believes that justice advocacy is the way to achieve participatory democracy. Similarly, while not tying service learning as closely to justice advocacy as does Mendel-Reyes, Rimmerman (1997a), considers justice advocacy to be the heart of participatory democracy, what he calls "the new citizenship" (p. 4). To be fair, Rimmerman includes community building as part of the new citizenship. But then, again, he says, "The New Citizenship is reflected in unconventional protest politics that mobilize the citizenry against the forces of corporate capitalism and the attempt to fight gender, racial and sexuality discrimination. He considers service learning to be an important ally in this struggle. Finally, while many faculty service-learning advocates mainly operate direct-service issues, they would like to move service learning to a justice model. The problem with the justice advocacy approach lies not so much in its goals as in its methodology, which typically is founded on conceptions of weak democracy.

The foundational similarity between academic traditionalism and the justice approach should be noted. Both base their theory on weak democracy or procedural republican thinking. Both ground their values in the autonomous individual. However, they differ, as I suggested, as to which human attribute is most worthy of developing. Whereas the traditionalist favors individual liberty, the justice advocate focuses on equality. As I have indicated, traditionalists within higher education usually favor learning for its own sake. I discuss this view further in the final chapter. However, some traditionalists see that higher education needs to be more socially responsible (Bok, 1990; Gutmann, 1987); yet they do not primarily see this endeavor involving greater community and campus partnerships, as I shall be discussing in relation to the commonwealth or civic republican version. Bok (1990), for example, advocates that institutions of higher education should engage in research aimed at addressing our urgent social concerns and maintains that colleges and universities should provide a greater effort to educate students morally. Gutmann also believes that a primary goal of higher education should be helping students improve their capacity for ethical and civic deliberation. Individual inequality and class stratification are objects of greatest concern.

Although educational traditionalists and justice advocates base their thinking on weak democratic principles, these two approaches differ sharply as to how one should go about addressing our urgent social concerns. As I have suggested, progressive traditionalists, such as Bok and Gutmann, favor moral education and civic deliberation. Justice advocates, who do not practice service learning, mainly rely on critical inquiry as a means of educating individuals to bring about social transformation. Although not all justice advocates support service learning, those who do, support this pedagogy as a means of getting students more connected with the community and more knowledgeable about social inequities. Service learning should deepen student commitment to social advocacy.

THE NEO-MARXIST THEORY OF JUSTICE

Some of the most fruitful thinking in terms of the justice approach has been critical pedagogy, especially in the work of Apple (1979, 1982/1985, 1989) and Giroux (1983,1988a, 1988b), which draws upon Marxist theory in attempting to provide a comprehensive analysis of the ways in which education, rather than serving as an approach to help achieve greater equality, serves to reinforce inequality by reproducing a class-divided society. The critical pedagogy approach provides, at minimum, a correction to noncritical pedagogy advocates of social justice. Many justice advocates in the service-learning movement tend to believe that drawing students into justice issues in the name of service is sufficient to motivate students to work in behalf of the elimination of social injustice. This approach simply underestimates the hegemonic power of education. When students, who may be from affluent universities, become involved in service, their work on behalf of eliminating social injustice often is qualified by a recognition of how this approach appears to call into question their own privileged positions. Affluent students begin to distance themselves from this approach at this point of recognition. At the very least, familiarity with the work of neo-Marxists thinkers such as Giroux and Apple will benefit justice advocates of service learning. Nevertheless, the neo-Marxist or critical pedagogy approach is problematic, because of its often unacknowledged connection with weak democracy. I comment on this shortly. First, I briefly summarize the neo-Marxist form of analysis and then suggest some difficulties this form of analysis as the methodology of service learning.

As I have suggested, critical pedagogy enlists education in the service of social transformation. In terms of this viewpoint, the hegemonic nature of society represents one of the main obstacles to social transformation. Marx has stated that the dominant class's ideas constitute the dominant ideas of the society. Material acquisition is the dominant value in the corporate capitalist society. Although other values exist, such as freedom and even spirituality, people often use these values in support of materialism or as a way to avoid challenges to materialist values.

For example, in our society the affluent frequently focus on spirituality. People pursue new-age religion, eastern religions, contemplation, and the like. While it is important to deepen one's spiritual life, this form of spiritual search often represents an attempt to create a privatized form of spirituality, which in fact, rationalizes one's position of power and class domination. Consider, for example, an affluent professional. This individual becomes consumed with an inner quest of spirituality that places a priority of meaning on this search and neglects the acknowledgment that part of what may have prompted the spiritual pilgrimage is really not a "spiritual" need, but rather a sense of emptiness aggravated by this individual's consumerist life-style. Attempts at spirituality can not really remove this emptiness. Instead, the person needs to confront the conditions of social inequality that underlie this life-style. As the example suggests, the dominant class noes not intentionally impose its values on everyone else. Rather, the political economy reinforces materialist values and the commidification of life. How does it do this?

Because this book mainly focuses on education and civic literacy, I illustrate the educational aspects of hegemony. To understand the hegemonic role of education, one needs first to understand the notion of bad faith. Bad faith is the tendency of the oppressed or the marginalized to take on or aspire to the values of the oppressors or the affluent class. The middle class is problematic, because this class is at once the oppressor and the oppressed. Members of the middle-class become oppressors as they support a political economy that economically suppresses and marginalizes a significant portion of people in our society, the working poor and the underclass. At the same time, a political economy that concentrates wealth in the hands of relatively few in our society, in effect oppresses the middle class.

It would be expected, from a neo-Marxist perspective, that eventually the oppressed would grow tired of their condition of subordination and rise up and overthrow those responsible for their social condition. But this radical response has not happened in our society. Why hasn't it? Hegemony subdues the subordinate classes as they assume the values of the dominant class. Education is one of the ways that bad faith is hegemonically reinforced.

The media constitutes one of the ways that our society exercises its hegemonic influence. Television programming provides entertainment that appeals to the lowest common denominator. For example, television programs have an overabundance of sitcoms that, through the use of humor, reinforce apolitical and simplistic views of life. Examples include the view that human relations consists mainly of one-liners, that people get themselves into trouble through humorous misadventure, and that laughter itself is the most important value in life. Soap operas focus on human beings preoccupied with sexual adventure and materialist, consumerist values. Talk shows focus on troubled relationships, through which viewers gain vicarious thrills by learning about the most private of affairs, involving sexual scandals and philandering (without public limits, privacy is trivialized). National networks focus on one sensational crime after another with no analysis of the underlying causes of these crimes. Telecasting positive social events often reinforces the perception that individual acts of charity are the most valuable responses to problems in our society. The local news media portray a society of violence where little good takes place except for local network-sponsored charities.

Individuals who live unfulfilled lives, often struggling economically, seek escape from the grim realities of their lives through television and other distractions. As they watch television, they identify ever more strongly with materialistic, consumer values that imprison them in their position of subordination. Through television, they live the vicarious life of the televised version of the American dream in all its tawdriness. Television does not intentionally adopt this role. The political economy creates this purpose. As one television critic has put it, commercial television sells products. Entertaining shows create a captive audience for commercials. Television shows appeal to the lowest common dominator because television stations want to sell products to the widest audience possible.

Formal education also is hegemonic, according to neo-Marxists, through a hidden curriculum that reinforces class division (Apple, 1979; Bennett and LeCompte, 1990; Giroux, 1981). One famous study (Anyon, 1988) highlighted the correspondence between the form of education and the class position of the students. For example, teachers in a middle school attended mainly by students from working-class backgrounds treated these students in ways that reinforced working-class values. Teachers viewed students as passive receptacles of knowledge and conditioned them to respect authority. Teachers placed little emphasis on empowering individual autonomy. In contrast, teachers in a predominantly middle-class school adopted a more student-centered approach to learning Similarly, teachers in an elite school used a discovery approach to learning, preparing students occupy positions of economic and professional leadership. This approach to learning emphasizes the role of the learner in arriving at solutions to problems.

In terms of the neo-Marxist perspective, the primary hegemonic function of formal education promotes the reproduction of class-consciousness, that is the creation of a set of attitudes, beliefs, and behaviors that ensure class division. The formal and the informal curriculum reproduces class-consciousness. Teachers promote values conducive to class reproduction. For example, social studies uphold the values of the neoconservative ideology, analyzing social problems in privatistic terms. Events are viewed as happening in a random way, rather than being a product of a particular kind of political economy. Teachers interpret history as mainly dealing with important events and important people, instead of helping students understand how history is constructed in ways that privilege some groups over others, such as males over females, one ethnic group over another.

Teachers encourage students to believe that they will be guaranteed economic mobility through hard work in school, a viewpoint that flies in the face of job market realities. In fact, only so my people can obtain a job within any particular occupation. When the supply exceeds the demand, the job market does not expand to accommodate the expanding pool of candidates. Sometimes as the result of an increased supply, in line with the market economy, wages go down as people within a particular occupation become increasingly expendable. In some cases, when a career becomes saturated, the educational system curtails this growth through credentialing. This has occurred in a number of occupations, such as social work and the health care industry.

Bowles and Gintis (1976) claim that the structure of social relations in education inures the student to the discipline of the workplace and develops the types of personal demeanor, modes of self-presentation, self-image, and social-class identifications, crucial ingredients of job adequacy (p. 131). For example, the social relationships of education—the relationships between administrators and teachers, teachers and students, students and students, and students and their work—replicate the hierarchical division of labor (p. 131).

Bowles and Gintis argue that education supports corporate capitalism by maintaining a large pool of available workers, thereby minimizing the prospect of strikes and other forms of labor agitation and protest. Whether intentional or not, the abundant supply of college graduates serves this economic purpose very well. Additionally, formal education serves as an institution that legitimizes and perpetuates hierarchical positions of power by ensuring that people at the top must have the "right" credentials and attend the "right" schools. Bowles and Gintis write: "The educational system legitimates economic inequality by providing an open, objective, and ostensibly merit ocratic mechanism for assigning individuals to unequal economic positions. The educational system fosters and reinforces the belief that economic success depends essentially on the possession of technical and cognitive skills which it is organized to provide in an efficient, equitable, and unbiased manner on the basis of meritocratic principle. The educational meritocracy is largely symbolic" (p. 103). Formal education tends to reproduce class division by providing a form of education that prepares students to accept their class-based position in society, while mass entertainment promotes bad faith, or attitudes in which people take a critical look at the political and economic structure that perpetuates this kind of inequitable class division.

THE FACULTY ROLE

The faculty role for the liberal or activist perspective is rather straightforward. The faculty have a particular responsibility to confront students with the reality of pervasive social inequality and to attempt to transform the consciousness of students, instilling in them a desire to work for social change aimed at reducing or eliminating social inequality and injustice.

A certain nostalgia exists among such faculty, who often look back at the civil rights movement and the Vietnam War protests as examples of the profound effect on society that justice education can achieve. Many college students were caught up in these two issues, lending some credence to the view that, at least in principle, education can play the role of contributing to the mobilization of students around such justice issues. However, caution is in order. In the first place, non-academic forces launched these movements, especially the civil rights movement. The Southern Christian Leadership Conference, led by Martin Luther King, Jr., was primarily responsible for creating the activist strategies of non-resistance style of protest, involving busing, marching, and sit-ins. Students respond to what they were observing in society, rather than to what they were learning in the class room or from radical or liberal professors. Another way of putting this is that students responded to overwhelming perceptions of inequality in a gut level form of social opposition. Why haven't there been similar student responses to the forms of inequality manifested by poverty and inequality? Here I think the answer becomes somewhat complex and also highlights the limitation of the more direct, activist version of social justice modes of education. In the first place, poverty, while obvious in a society, is difficult to analyze. For example, while segregationist policies caused the plight of blacks in the Jim-Crow South, the plight of people in poverty is not so easily attributable to overt policies of "discrimination." Clearly, an "economic system" that produces so many people in poverty is faulty. But widespread disagreement exists over how to analyze this problem and what to do about it. It is, of course, here that the activist has a role to play. Unfortunately, student apathy and economically motivated resistance thwarts the activist professor's desire to help his or her students comprehend the underlying social forces or causes of poverty. And so the activist professor becomes frustrated. Why can't students rise to the cause of combating poverty with the same enthusiasm that students in the past rose up against the war and racism?

It is here that the neo-Marxist analysis asserts itself. The neo-Marxist is attuned to the hegemonic role of education. For all of the reasons cited above, it seems difficult politically to affect or alter the consciousness of students. Due to cultural hegemony, students tend to shy away from structural analysis. Moreover, as I have suggested, in the absence of societal models or examples, college students who themselves are preparing to take their place in the hierarchical world of work as managers and professionals seem resistant to accepting a form of social analysis that, by implication, challenges their future aspirations in the work force.

However, two related problems exist with the neo-Marxist analysis. In the first place, thinkers such as Bowles and Gintis argue that education primarily serves the purpose of reproducing class division. And while education can play a role in critically challenging the reproductive role of education, the fundamental change needed is a more democratic economy, through greater democratic socialization and worker control of the means of production.

By the same token, neo-Marxists, such as Giroux (1981) and Apple (1979) have maintained that Bowles and Gintis fail to understand the degree to which hegemony, rather than market demands, shapes education. Giroux seems to place more faith in the possibility that educational institutions, through critical pedagogy, can make students more conscious of hegemony and therefore be poised to work for social change. Critical pedagogy teaches students to be more self-conscious of their class position in society, and ways in which the dominant values of society disempower them in their learning.

As far as I am concerned, the approaches of Bowles and Gintis and Apple and Giroux are both needed—there, indeed, must be a critical pedagogical effort to help students become more transformative in their work. Unfortunately, the neo-Marxist approach, in my opinion, focuses to much on teaching as the medium of social transformation. This is an overly intellectualized approach. Middle-class students, and others, must experience the conditions of injustice which are the object of intellectual analysis.

In fact, one could argue that the neo-Marxist class room based approach represents an unwillingness of the radical professor to become a public intellectual. Railing against the evils of society from the lectern and remaining in one's class room or in one's office writing articles and books, instead of also becoming engaged in the community, may in itself constitute another devise of the hidden curriculum. The professor portrays himself or herself as exempt, by virtue of his or her intellectual role, from praxis, from becoming personally and professionally engaged in socially transformative work. The radical professor mouths radical platitudes, but, in fact, functions as a member of the professional class, unintentionally reinforcing class stratification and political and economic inequality—the very opposite of what the professor desires. Public intellectuals are not merely those who teach critical pedagogy but are those who join with their students and fellow community members in attacking the problems which are the subject of their critical analysis. Combing service learning with critical pedagogy is an important step toward working for social transformation. Finally, justice professors who remain disconnected from community work tend to work on single issues, such as feminism or racism. Becoming involved in community development work enables professors and their students to understand the connection of all justice issues to condition is of the political economy.

Efforts also must be made to work for a greater democratic economy. Worker cooperatives, for example, are one of the most promising models of community economic development. Nonprofit community development organizations also are vital to helping economically transform low-income communities. I discuss these forms of economic development in Chapter 9. Critical pedagogy is useful in training people in how to develop and operate cooperatives. In particular, people bring into worker cooperatives the values of hierarchial workplaces, such as a tendency to not trust one another and to not work cooperatively. Of course, the political economy itself exacerbates our competitive nature. We all tend to adopt very privatized approaches to life.

Working in the community to develop alternative democratic economic can create transformative work. If students become engaged in this kind of work through community service, this can help them become more liberated from hegemony and to be more committed to a more just society with greater economic equality. But how do we deal with student resistance to this effort? I believe that service learning is a good way to go about this work, but I believe we must go beyond the justice model.

THE JUSTICE MODEL OF SERVICE LEARNING

Justice activists are understandably attracted to service learning. They are so, first, for some of the same reasons that voluntarists are. Service learning promotes moral development among students. Service learning also develops social consciousness among students. Again, our pervasive social problems of homelessness, poverty, and discrimination discourage students from believing they can counteract these trends. Service learning becomes a means that enables students—and faculty for that matter—to find pathways into the community and to become involved in social issues. Students may become socially transformed through working at homeless shelters or on environmental issues.

Service learning also creates a means of engaging students with issues in the community. Students aiming for professional careers resist a more radical critique of society because they see their values as being criticized in the process. Certainly, this kind of resistance may persist even in the context of service learning, but it may be minimized with more community-involved activity. This may happen because as students become engaged with those in poverty, for example, students may discover the humanity of the people with whom they are dealing. They may discover that in some sense we all are "marginalized" in our society by the current system. They in effect may be transformed by this kind of work.

This kind of transformation will not happen just as a by-product of the service experience. It is important, as is often emphasized within the service-learning movement, that faculty provide guided reflection on students' service experience in which the relevance of course content to the community issues is explored. Students must confront and analyze issues of inequality. By this means students will deepen their understanding of the issues with which they are engaged.

So far at least in the service-learning movement, I do not think we see much evidence that a revival of student activism has attended service learning. Of course, students become involved in local causes, but often these causes involve direct-delivery service models. For example, students might get involved in a fund raiser for a homeless family or for some other local charity. But there does not seem to be any widespread activist movement resulting. Why is this?

Several factors inhibiting transformative progress include a lack of a pedagogical procedure justifying activist work and a lack of community development models of service learning. In terms of a lack of a pedagogical procedure, a case can be made that we need to honor the principle of liberal neutrality in classroom instruction. Traditionalist critics of activism are correct in this regard. Students need to consider all significant alternative opinions or points of view. It is difficult for a professor to assign students to such a task as to advocate for gay rights through a gay rights organization. Some students may not wish to do this; they may be opposed to gay rights. If a professor says that all students who wish to advocate on behalf of gay rights should do so, then the professor may be end up marginalizing students who are opposed to gay rights. Because of these problems, the civic model of service learning is better suited for achieving these kinds of goals.

In the absence of a community development model of service learning, students usually end up providing direct delivery of service and never end working for social change, despite professorial justice advocacy. This becomes another problem. For example, students interested in the plight of homeless people, rather than getting involved in a community-based organization advocating on behalf of homeless people, usually end up working in a homeless shelter serving meals in the soup kitchen, a form of direct service. Therefore, an alternative model of service learning may help mitigate these problems. I believe that the civic model provides a corrective. I do want to say that a community development service learning requires the civic model of service learning. But the civic model minimum addresses the issue of liberal neutrality. I shall discuss this in the next chapter.

THE SOCIAL JUSTICE VIEW OF CIVIC LITERACY

I have claimed that the justice viewpoint as violating the principle of liberal neutrality. While this is not so much of a problem for private educational institutions dedicated to a particular justice cause, this is a serious problem for public institutions of education. So the educational challenge becomes that of attempting to determine a process by which faculty and students can address justice issues in a way that honors or acknowledges the principle of liberal neutrality. As I have indicated, I believe that the civic literacy approach accomplishes this. I discuss this in the following chapter.

The deeper problem with the neo-Marxist and other versions of the justice approach is its embeddedness in weak democracy or philosophical liberalism. This approach lacks a vision of the good life and also assumes that justice is mainly a zero-sum matter of redistributing economic goods more equitably. Of course, any society that is worthy of the appellation "just" would strive for an equitable distribution of economic goods. But focusing on the issue of fair distribution is problematic.

In the first place, the zero-sum model assumes that the primary good is economic. However, other values are equally as important, such as a sense of community, the opportunity for individual creativity, and spiritual development. True, talking about a society where creativity can flourish is mere rhetoric to those individuals who do not posses the basic necessities of life. But we should not overlook the importance of working to create a more holistic society.

In the second place, creating opportunities for people to develop more holistically may be necessary to realize a more just economy. Certainly, through advertisement and the media our society reinforces the notion that we primarily should concern ourselves with material consumption. Also, people turn to consumerism to appease empty and alienated lives. At times it is as important for educators to promote creative and spiritual development as it is to work for economic justice. This is the case, because a good society or community provides opportunities for self-development, not only economically, but personally, ethically, and spiritually. Unfortunately, all too often creative and spiritual development works not as part of a holistic approach to personal liberation and social change, but as an escape from alienation and a rationalization of the privatized conditions that our society has promoted in the evisceration of our sense of the public. These considerations have a direct bearing on the economy. We need to recover a sense of the spirituality of work, as emphasized by Fox (1994). However, this sense of the importance of spirituality can not obfuscate the need to work for achieving more democratic forms of work, such as cooperatives. The two must go hand in hand.

The justice approach ironically may undermine its goal of achieving a more just society. It does so through the assumption that we are privatized individuals intent upon maximizing self-interests and that the primary means of achieving a more just society is through wresting from the haves more of the economic pie for the have nots. The desire for greater economic justice is not the fault of this conceptual model. The underlying assumption of privatized self-interest upon which the model is predicated constitutes the fault.

Weak democracy ideology, in my opinion, also reinforces the justice oriented professor's tendency to engage in single-issue advocacy. Professors champion their pet causes, such as feminism, the environment, and racism, failing to acknowledge the structural interdependence of all such issues. Also, I have mentioned that justice professors who remain aloof from community developmental work also are susceptible to this tendency as well.

In terms of the commonwealth or citizen democracy approach that underlies the civic model, individuals are primarily social beings who can achieve self-realization and fulfillment only in the context of community. Therefore individuals have a vested self-interest in community growth and sustainment. Adopting this perspective helps us realize that working for social change and greater economic justice must take place within an approach to social and community development that attends to a diverse range of personal needs, including economic, but also spiritual and creative. I turn in the next chapter to an elaboration of the commonwealth or citizen democracy model.

7

Service Learning and Strong Democracy

Although civic indifference abounds in our society, many people express interest in becoming more involved politically in their local communities. Matthews (1994) discusses the Harwood study of *Citizens and Politics: A View from Main Street America* (Harwood Group, 1991) done by the Kettering Foundation of which David Matthews is the president. This study found citizens not apathetic, according to the conventional wisdom, but angry over their sense of powerlessness and exclusion. They also share deep political concerns and an untapped sense of civic duty. The study also found that "the key to civic participation for those who participated was not the certainty of control or success but the possibility of change. Americans seem to overcome the obstacles to participation when they believe that they might have an effect—that there is some opportunity to create and witness change" (Matthews, 1994, p. 36). The study also found that self-interest does not always equal selfish interest: "People have a self-interest in advancing the broader public interest" (p. 62). While seldom captured by the national news, there have been hundreds of examples of citizen action in support of fair-housing and lending practices, against environmental pollution, neighborhood cleanup, and job development. This form of participatory democracy provides the context for extending our understanding of service learning to incorporate community development initiatives. Following are some examples of this kind of effort.

A collaborative effort between The University of Louisville, local government, business, and community organizations has revitalized Russell, a low-income neighborhood in Louisville, Kentucky (Gilderbloom et al.,

1997). The University of Louisville received a U.S. Department of Education Urban Community Service Program grant, Housing and Neighborhood Development Strategies (HANDS) in 1992. The university worked in close partnership with the community to build the capacity of organizations and individuals to revitalize Russell and leverage limited local funds through grants and other sources to provide capital or access to capital for many ventures in the community. "The cornerstone of the Russell Partnership is attracting moderate-income families to the neighborhood by providing opportunities for home ownership" (Gilderbloom et al., p. 43). There have been a number of accomplishments. Banks provide below-market financing, community groups organize nonprofit community development organizations, and churches are building housing for their members. "The Russell Partnership is also training residents to become housing contractors and to develop small businesses. Funds have been identified for a small-business loan program and business incubator for the Russell area" (Gilderbloom et al., p. 44). The crime rate in the neighborhoods undergoing revitalization and new home construction have dropped. "Russell is recycling the existing infrastructure of roads, sewage, utilities, and buildings to slow down imprudent development in the undeveloped outer metropolitan areas" (p. 45). New houses construction is vibrant, small businesses are thriving, and the first new urban park in years will be constructed.

Bullard (1997) writes of a two decade effort to dismantle environmental racism, which is defined as "any policy, practice, or directive that differentially affects (whether intended or unintended) individuals, groups, or communities based on race" (p. 68). Bullard provides substantial evidence that a disproportionate number of landfills and other environmentally dangerous facilities, such as nuclear power plants, have been located in predominately African American communities. He writes about his effort in the 1970s to halt the allocation of landfills in African American communities in Houston. This effort led to a significant national initiative to stop environmental racism. More recently, in Louisiana, local residents of two African American communities, Forest Grove and Center Springs, organized themselves into a group called CANT (Citizens Against Nuclear Trash), to halt the construction of the nation's first privately owned uranium enrichment plant.

Lappé and Du Bois (1994) tell the story of how the citizens' organization Allied Communities of Tarrant (ACT) influenced Texas Wesleyan College not to relocate out of a poor Fort Worth neighborhood. If the college pulled out, ACT feared the neighborhood had virtually no chance of recovery. "The campus provided the last point of stability on which to rebuild the neighborhood" (p. 53). ACT leader and members—mostly moderate- and low-income blacks, whites, and Hispanics—met with the board of trustees and the college's president. The group prepared by engaging in role play, according to the Reverend Terry Boggs, one of the leaders of ACT. As a result of this citizen effort the college re-committed itself to the community.

Lappé and Du Bois (1994) cite another interesting example of citizen action in Connecticut's Naugatuck Valley and Massachusetts' Merrimack Valley. Once a center of the nation's thriving brass industry, by the 1970s dozens of factories and plants had closed. Many communities were dying. Citizens concerned about what they could do to revitalize their communities formed the Naugatuck Valley Project (NVP), whose members include sixty-eight religious, union, community, and business organizations. "Their goal (and that of NVP's sister project, the Merrimack Valley Project in eastern Massachusetts) is ambitious: 'to create new democratic institutions as models of how we can restructure our society'" (p. 103). From citizen efforts have grown the worker-owned Valley Care Cooperative Home Care company modeled after New York's successful Cooperative Home Health Care. They also have created a land trust that has already generated one hundred units of permanently affordable housing. NVP also defeated a city plan to replace a park with an incinerator.

Kretzmann and McKnight (1993) provide countless examples of individual, community, and institutional efforts to improve community life. Here are a few examples:

- In a rural community, a group of citizens created a locally owned and operated radio station. This station is available to local individuals and associations to broadcast debates, announcements, and performances. "The station is the 'voice' of the community" (p. 133).
- A group of unemployed public housing residents formed an association to seek jobs. "They created a job service that helped prepare members for jobs and referred residents to permanent and part-time job opportunities" (p. 133). Over 75 residents have secured jobs.
- A group of neighborhood block clubs joined together to inventory the skills and capabilities of the residents of the area. The group has initiated self-help, mutual support and exchange networks. "They have also created a property management cooperative that employees the skills of local residents to provide services to landlords in the neighborhood" (p. 133).

These kinds of community development efforts are examples of what Boyte (1996) calls the commonwealth tradition and Barber (1984) calls strong or participatory democracy. Rimmerman (1997a) calls this activity the new citizenship.[1] Citing the Harwood Group student study (1993), Rimmerman (1997a) concludes that students can imagine a different politics. This different politics, rooted in bringing people together at the community level, finds ways to talk and act on problems. Through service learning efforts, students are becoming involved in supporting community-building efforts. I discuss examples of these activities in Chapter 9.

Unfortunately, Rimmerman fails to draw a distinction between advocacy politics, characteristic of Alinsky's work, and more broadly based community development work. Surely, community development work at times requires advocacy, which some of the above examples illustrate. But other forms of community work, including economic development seem necessary to become a truly functioning democratic society. As I claimed in the previous chapter, the civic republican tradition and weak democracy or classical liberalism tradition fosters a difference between advocacy politics and a broader community-building effort. The weak democracy basis of justice advocacy fosters a zero-sum mentality, which encourages advocacy and conflict as the initial option rather the court of last resort. On the other hand, the civic republican philosophy promotes the holistic development of the community, including political economic development. This latter outlook, I believe, encourages people, not to abandon the liberal ideals of liberty and justice, but to recognize that creating sustainable democratic communities will enable these values to flourish. Strong democracy promotes building holistic or healthy communities instead of advocating on behalf of special interest needs, such as diversity, gay rights, and environmental protection—although all of these concerns must be addressed in the context of community development.

Participatory democracy must not necessarily be based on a liberal communitarian foundation. Some people work for a more just and healthy community out of pragmatic reasons or even out of an intuitive sense that this effort is simply the right thing to do. People do not always engage in political work on the basis of a theoretical perspective. And I have no quarrel with such individual motivations for working on behalf of the common good. As Rorty (1989/1997) observes: "The idea that liberal societies are bound together by philosophical beliefs seems to me ludicrous. What binds societies together are common vocabularies and common hopes" (p. 86).

However, theoretical justification, I believe, is helpful to provide a deeper understanding of why participatory democracy involves more than advocacy politics. The legacy of weak democracy or classical liberalism has tended to obscure the importance of creating sustainable democratic communities that enable the liberal values of liberty and justice to be achieved and flourish. Because the hegemony of classical liberalism or weak democracy is so strong in our political thinking, it is difficult at times to understand what is missing in this philosophy. A better understanding of the public philosophy of civic republicanism or liberal communitarianism, and its civic virtues enables us to focus more clearly on the importance of developing sustainable democratic communities as places where liberty and justice flourishes. Finally, the implications of this philosophy for service learning must be clarified.

Historically, the strong democracy, or commonwealth view has been overshadowed by the weak democracy or the procedural republic view. Sandel (1996) has provided a very informative view of the history of the eclipse of the commonwealth view by the "procedural republic." Sandel points out that historically a tension existed between two versions of public philosophy, procedural republicanism and civic republican theory. Procedural republicanism emphasized that freedom consists in our capacity to choose our ends for ourselves. This theory also maintains that government "should not affirm, through its policies or laws, any particular conception of the good life; instead it should provide a neutral framework of rights within which people can choose their own values and ends" (p. 58).[2] In contrast, civic republican or strong democracy theory emphasized the notion that liberty depends on sharing in self-government. Sandel points out that self-government is not by itself inconsistent with liberal freedom. "Participating in politics can be one among the ways in which people choose to pursue their individual ends" (p. 58). However, for civic republican theory sharing in self-rule also involves "deliberating with fellow citizens about the common good and helping to shape the destiny of the political community" (p. 58). Accomplishing this goal involves more than the capacity to choose one's ends and to respect others' rights to do the same. "It requires a knowledge of public affairs and also a sense of belonging, a concern for the whole, a moral bond with the community worse fate is at stake" (p. 58).

Early on, Thomas Jefferson expressed the civic republican philosophy in advocating that the new republic should maintain an agrarian way of life and discouraging industrial manufacturing. He feared that large-scale manufacturing would undermine the independence required for republican citizenship. However, Jefferson's views did not prevail. The tension between the two public philosophies has extended throughout our history, especially during the Civil War and the Progressive Era. The debate took different forms. But the concern always existed regarding the growth of industrialization, and later, of corporate power in relation to self-government. The civic republican strand of the argument dealt with the civic consequences of industrial and corporate power. On the other hand, the procedural republican perspective emphasized the importance of individual freedom and tended to locate the root of the social problems in governmental restrictions on industrial and corporate power.

The Progressive Era concerned itself especially with the preservation of democratic government in the face of growing industrialization. However, in contemporary times, the shift has occurred toward concern about the maximization of economic growth and distributive justice.

According to Sandel, the Keynesian emphasis on the maximization of economic growth and distributive justice marked the demise of the civic republican strand of republicanism and the rise of procedural republicanism or contemporary liberalism. Again, according to this form of liberalism, "government should be neutral as to conceptions of the good life, in order to respect persons as free and independent selves, capable of choosing their own ends" (p. 66) In these terms, the liberal project was to use federal power "to vindicate individual rights that local communities had failed to protect" (p. 69). In contrast, the neoconservative reaction, especially under President Ronald Reagan, evoked certain civic republic themes, such as the value of the family and the local community, and criticized the federal government as the culprit for what ailed us. At the same time, Reagan and other neoconservatives failed to point out the ways in which corporate excess has served to undermine local moral and civic values. Sandel observes of Reagan: "The unfettered capitalism he favored did nothing to repair the moral fabric of families, neighborhoods, and communities and much to undermine them" (p. 69).

CRITIQUE OF WEAK DEMOCRACY

I have criticized civic republicanism or weak democracy in several preceding chapters. Before proceeding to dwell on a defense of strong democracy and its relationship to service learning, I shall briefly repeat the fundamental criticisms of the weak democracy approach.

In the first place, weak democracy operates from an assumption of the privatized individual, that we are primarily motivated by self-interest and a selfish form of self-interest to boot. This outlook usually generates some form of social contractarian theory of social justice. If we assume that we are fundamentally privatized self-interested individuals, tending to selfishness, it would seem that the primary reason for organizing as a community or society would be for mutual self-protection. But this viewpoint fails, in my opinion, in not recognizing that we are essentially social beings in which our recognition of the value and dignity of others and the value of making decisions in the interest of the common good emerges through the dialogical language process from childhood. As we master a natural language, we necessarily assume that we ought to treat others with value and dignity. This assumption comes with the acquisition of the concept of "personhood."

Second, the weak democracy approach tends to focus on individual development at the expense of the development of community and the common good. An example of this extreme perspective is expressed by Rorty (1989/1997): "A liberal society is one whose ideals can be fulfilled by persuasion rather than force, by reform rather than revolution, by the free and open encounters of present linguistic and other practices with suggestions for new practices. But this is to say than an ideal liberal society is one which has no purpose except freedom, no goal except a willingness to see how such encounters go and to abide by the outcome" (p. 60). While perhaps not endorsed by Rorty, support of the corporate capitalist economy flows from the concept of the excessive value of individuality and autonomy. Giving capitalism the greatest freedom possible, it is believed, will automatically work to our common betterment.

Barber (1984), in his critique of "thin democracy"—I use the phrase "weak democracy" instead—maintains that this form of democracy has outlived its usefulness. Whereas at one point in the development of democracy, emphasis upon liberty as a hedge against despotism was perhaps a natural political step, this emphasis has become pathological. It now is contributing to the molding of mass men, "individuals defined by their privacy and their property yet unable to determine who they are, emancipated by rights and freedoms but unable to act as morally autonomous agents, driven by ambition and lust yet distanced from their happiness by the very powers that were supposed to facilitate it achievement" (pp. 97–98).

Thus, individuality begins to lose its meaning when it is abstracted from the community context that imbues individuality with meaning. The same applies to the notion of liberty or autonomy. Barber claims that self-direction achieves freedom only when the self is emancipated from impulse and appetite and when the self is associated with intention and purposes that by their nature only can arise within the guiding limits of a society and a culture (p. 100).

This theory that was supposed to defend individuals from power. However, the effect of the emptiness of the individual from the perspective of philosophical liberalism or weak democracy, strips them of the social armor by which they could defend themselves (p. 101). Philosophical liberalism or weak democracy undermines democracy, leaving us more vulnerable to totalitarianism. Barber writes:

A society that centralizes power in the name of liberty but at the cost of self-government, and that at the same time pursues the rhetoric of pure individualism and absolute freedom without providing for a politically free citizenry, is a society ripe for both anarchy *and* tyranny—or for that rapid succession from the former to the latter that has typified some of the past century's ill-fated experiments in thin democracy. (p. 104)

Pratte (1988a) in a similar vein, maintains that changes in the U.S. economy vitiates philosophical liberalism as a democratic social theory. This theory of democracy presumes a symmetry between economic individual advancement and aggregate effects. The neoconservative version of philosophical liberalism supported supply-side economics, with the presumed trickle-down effect on social and economic improvement. Unfortunately, the opposite resulted.

Supply-side economics under Reagan and Bush resulted in a quadrupling of the national debt, from one to four trillion dollars. Rather than assuring general prosperity, this individualistic logic in the economy has resulted in an increasing gap between the haves and the have-nots. One quarter of American children are in poverty. Capital is being exported abroad, especially to Third World countries, displacing American workers from higher paying factory jobs. In an era of low unemployment, we are mainly seeing growth in the lower paying service sector. We also are experiencing growth in part-time employment with fewer benefits. Corporate downsizing has eroded the belief in permanency of corporate employment and consequently has lessened corporate loyalty.

Pratte writes, "the consequences of laissez-faire economics are nasty and brutal for many disadvantaged Americans, such as the homeless, the aged, unorganized laborers, the black, underclass, the disabled, and increasingly, white-collar workers whose skills have become outdated" (p. 39). Add to these Rifkin's (1995) prediction that in the future even more jobs will be eliminated because of computerization, then we can recognize that there is an urgent need for greater accountability of the economy to the public. But of course, weak democracy is not equipped to accommodate this need.

I have already stated this, but it bears repeating in this context. The individualist philosophy often looks to education as the mechanism for social advancement. And, certainly, we can look to individual examples of people who have achieved social advancement due to education. This is true for all ethnic groups. And individual successes support a convenient myth that "all people can improve their lives, if only they will work hard." Unfortunately, the structure of our economy refutes this myth. Educational inflation undermines the belief that individual effort is rewarded by economic success. There are only so many people who can become successful professionals, for example. Some people simply remain underemployed as the result of an oversupply among the professional.

Pratte also claims that, as a normative social theory, philosophical liberalism or civic republicanism projects an ethic of independence an individualism no longer in keeping with the reality of global interdependence and mutual dependence. For example, it frames the ecological critique as a threat to personal freedom (p. 39). But we realize that ecologically we can not have our cake and eat it too. Protecting our environment for future generations requires hard choices that often involve conflicts between jobs and the environment, as we have witnessed in the debates about saving the spotted owl in the northwestern part of the United States. Unfortunately, it is the very limitation of the zero-sum philosophy of the social contract approach that artificially limits the framework of such debates. A more community-oriented approach would begin to look holistically at providing other forms of employment for loggers. But such an approach would require different forms of response than those available from the perspective of weak democracy.

Pratte concludes that, as a political ideology, weak democracy fosters a strongly individualistic form of competition that weakens a much-needed sense of civic compassion and decency. Perhaps no person better epitomizes this than Donald Trump, who attempts to make a virtue of his egoism. Americans who support economic politics that benefit the wealthy at the expense of the middle and lower levels out of the misguided belief that this is necessary if everyone is to have the opportunity to become a billionaire should ask themselves the question, is Donald Trump what they want to become? Is that the image of the kind of individual we uphold as a virtuous American?

STRONG DEMOCRACY

The work of writers such as Barber (1984, 1992), Bellah and associates (1985, 1991), Boyte (1989), Pratte (1988a, 1988b), Sandel (1982, 1996, 1996, March), Selznick (1992), Sullivan (1982), and Taylor (1989, 1991, 1992, 1994), in my opinion, are each in their own way reclaim different aspects of the civic republican tradition. Each of these writers would not necessarily agree that the others represent the same "tradition." However, I think they are. Boyte, at least in his latest writings, emphasizes the importance of the creation of "public work" as essential to the establishment of a basis for local self-government. Barber emphasizes the importance of thoughtful deliberation among active citizens. Sandel stresses the importance of moral community building. Taylor provides an analysis of how we need to return to the building of the local moral community as a hedge against technological manipulation.

Dewey's thought (1927/1954) certainly supports this tradition. As far back as the 1920s, Dewey was concerned about what he called the "eclipse of the public." He noted that elected officials did not feel responsible to the public, and the public itself was civically apathetic. He believed that the injection of technological forces in the service of capitalism distorted the civic process. Excessive economic individualism increased the economic power of the capitalistic class. For Dewey, creating the "great community" would dilute the concentration of power was to create the "great community." He says, "The cure for the ailments of democracy is more democracy" (1927/1954, p. 146). Dewey adds, "Democracy is not an alternative to other principles of associated life. It is the idea of community life itself" (p. 148). A more citizen driven democracy would recognize that fraternity, liberty, and equality isolated from communal life devoted to sustaining the common good are hopeless abstractions (p. 149).

Boyte and Farr (1997) surface what they consider to be an important difference between the commonwealth tradition and communitarianism. They consider communitarianism to focus too exclusively on the community, the building of moral consensus. They also believe that the model of service learning that seems to match this community orientation is the volunteer approach. In fact, they believe that the AmeriCorps itself was animated by just such a communitarian orientation.

I agree that there are lines of communitarian thinking, especially in a writer such as Etzioni (1993) who can lead one to draw these conclusions about the shortcomings of communitarian thinking. However, I think it is too soon to write the final chapter to the development of communitarianism. A strong philosophical justification for this theory has not yet been produced. I, for example, have suggested in various places that I consider myself to be a liberal communitarian. And this is not a statement of whether I am to the left or right on certain issues. I see the need for the development of a form of communitarianism that includes some aspects of philosophical liberalism and some aspects of communitarianism. The communitarian dimension should accommodate the notion that the unencumbered self of philosophical liberalism or weak democracy is untenable. We are, as writers such as Bellah and associates (1985), Selznick (1992), and Taylor (1989, 1991) argue, essentially social beings. Social relations and our social commitments provide find individual fulfillment. Taylor (1989) suggests that the very narrative conditions of language illuminates how individuals acquire moral understanding. And I am inclined in this direction of thinking as well. The narrative conditions of language, which might help ground morality, help us understand how we acquire "moral consciousness." But this is not a universal grounding in the Kantian tradition which unsuccessfully attempts to provide a rational foundation. A liberal communitarian theory should help us understand the importance of securing the common good, which is historically implicit within classical liberalism, but obscured by the concept of the procedural republic, as Sandel has documented (1996). Even Rawls (1971) recognizes this as he acknowledges that we need to adopt those practices of fairness that promote the greatest amount of opportunity for all concerned. But a complete defense of liberal communitarianism along these lines has not yet been developed.

Unfortunately, communitarian thinking often neglects the liberal virtues, especially the importance of our fundamental right to choose our own individual way of life. A robust communitarian perspective should cultivate both a sense of commitment to the common good and a sense of the importance of independence or liberty. For without self-development, one can not make intelligible decisions regarding the common good or anything else. Communitarian critics are certainly justified in being wary of an overemphasis on the overriding value of the common good as a basis of moral decision making. At the same time, I would argue that our very conception of the common good, forged in the narrative acquisition of natural language through communicative discourse in which we come to recognize the fundamental dignity and respect of others, includes society founded on the principles of liberty and fairness. In this respect, Rawls (1981) correctly insists on the primacy of liberty and fairness, although he unfortunately attempts to secure his concept of a good society in terms of a version of procedural liberalism. Although moral education may always reflect a tension between maximizing individual liberty and securing the common good, I agree with Rawls that liberty and fairness are essential planks in our very conception of the common good.

Promoting individual liberty is important for both liberal communitarianism and traditional philosophical liberalism. Unfortunately, philosophical liberalism maintains that we arrive at a sense of individual self-value independent of our connections with others, and thus fails to acknowledge the degree to which self-development is dependent on community development. For liberal communitarianism, liberty and fairness are grounded in the very same language-based communal source of values as the notion of the common good.

What I am calling liberal communitarian also parts company with communitarian thinkers, such as Sullivan (1989) and even a strong democracy thinker like Barber (1984), who advocate that in some sense the only basis for ethics lies in the values of community-based deliberation. We as member of a community make progress in civic deliberation and action through pragmatic procedures. But this form of decision making is not the basis of ethics. Without a deeper grounding in the values of liberty, fairness, and the common good, these very notions may be ignored in the heat of civic deliberation. The values of liberty, fairness and the common good form the bedrock set of social practices that inform moral education and civic deliberation. Thus, I agree with Benn and Peters (1959) that our conception of democracy is not majority rule but a political procedural process involving majority rule, having as it foundational principle upholding the common good in ways that include maximizing liberty and fairness.

I have attempted, in a suggestive way to lay out a case for what I call liberal communitarianism, because I think that writers like Boyte and Farr (1997) are right in being concerned that a bland evocation of the importance of community responsibility and community involvement can lead to a diminished sense of civic decision making. So in the interest of developing a stronger framework of philosophical support for the commonwealth tradition, I encourage greater debate and discussion of how we can clarify and refine the concept of the common good implicit within the concept of a liberal society. Writers in the strong democracy and commonwealth tradition that I have mentioned also fail to recognize that the development of economic democracy is at the core of the development of strong democracy. These writers are critical of corporate power as undermining the values of strong democracy, and they advocate that the main route to the development of the strong democracy tradition is through building community, a sense of the public, and greater local civic decision making. They fail to address the importance of creating economically sustainable democratic communities. As Harkavy points out (August, 1996), Barber (1992) emphasizes classroom-based civic education as the tool for civic consciousness raising, neglecting the importance of community development work. To his credit, Barber sees much value in service learning, although he fails to develop a community-development model.

By creating a more democratic economy, I mean addressing those aspects of work and the economy that have tended to erode our civic base. I find it interesting that Sandel (1996) traces the eclipse of the civic republican tradition by the procedural republic notion throughout the history of our country with little recognition that reviving the civic republican tradition involves first and foremost combating those aspects of the economy that are responsible for the demise of the republican tradition.

For example, there is little doubt that excessive corporate power contributes to civic disconnection. The market economy manipulates our society, creating a nation of consumers and ignoring the importance of the spiritual and communal values that sustain us both as a society and as individuals. Attacking the root problem, excessive corporate power, is clearly the only way we can address this multifaceted problem. Boyte (1989) highlights our rich populist tradition that we can draw upon to constrain corporate power.

Boyte and Kari (1996) have emphasized the importance of public work itself, where individuals come to see themselves as coproducers of something that is greater than the sum of the work of the individuals who create it. Certainly small businesses and home-based businesses are important as counter-measures to corporate economic centralization. Through creating their own businesses, individuals develop their own talents. Small businesses themselves, unfortunately, can also reinforce the individualist strain of thinking at the heart of the procedural republican concepts. So we can not look to small business development alone as an anodyne. And recently, in my opinion, there too much attention has been given to microenterprise or home-based business development as a way to provide jobs for welfare members being forced off the welfare rolls and a way to rebuild communities. Welfare recipients often lack the economic stability necessary for microenterprise development. Micro-enterprises also can reinforce the privatization of the economy, because individuals are busy operating home-based businesses, a form of work that does not necessarily promote democratic engagement. Nevertheless, small business and home-based business development comprise a counter-measure to corporate power and represents one pathway for community development and individual economic self-sufficiency.

Democratizing the workplace is one of the most needed efforts to constrain excessive corporate power and to contribute to greater civic advocacy. Writers such as Bowles and Gintis (1976) advocate this from the neo-Marxist perspective. Corporate America's trend in developing teamwork approaches to management and company operation is suspect. In some cases the teamwork approach may promote an authentic sense that employees are enabled to play a greater role in democratic decision making. However, as Rifkin (1995) points out, often teamwork is really being used as a cost-saving device to flatten the management structure and to eliminate middle-management, replacing managers with greater computerization and giving more authority to the shop floor employees. Unfortunately, workers are only given the appearance of democratic decision making. As long as they have more decision-making authority but no greater share of the economic rewards for their work, they still have little democratic control.

More encouraging developments are the emergence of Employee Stock Option Plans (ESOPS), companies in which employees take ownership through gaining a majority share of stocks. ESOPS abound throughout the country, and include such well-known companies as Avis and United Airlines. Some critics fault these companies as still being inequitable because those who command the largest salaries in the company are able to acquire more stocks and benefit more than those employees who earn smaller salaries. Nevertheless, the plethora of ESOPS has created a greater acceptance of the ideal of democratizing the workplace.

A related and, I believe, more important form of economic democracy is employee-owned businesses, or worker cooperatives. Worker cooperatives have had a difficult history. Most recently, in the late sixties and early seventies, a number of cooperatives emerged across the country. Many were in the food cooperative area, others in the plywood and steel industry. Worker- or employee-owned businesses operate according to democratic principles (Adams and Hansen, 1993). It is my firm belief, that as people experience democracy in the workplace, this will or can have a spillover effect in our lives outside of work. Conversely, as we experience little empowerment in the workplace, this can only reinforce our sense of helplessness at home and in the community.

Other forms of democratic work can include community-owned businesses (Gunn and Dayton, 1991), such as a neighborhood association owning and operating a grocery store, as is about to happen in Minneapolis. Another example is New Westside Economic Development Inc. (NEWSED), a predominately Hispanic community economic development nonprofit organization in Denver, Colorado, that owns a variety of small businesses, including a storage facility. I discuss this organization further in Chapter 9. And we must not forget our municipal and other public institutions, including education, vital sources of democracy in the workplace, even though many public institutions are run rather autocratically. This fact should not deter us from continuing to work to create these forms of democratic work.

As I have previously indicated, Lappé and Du Bois (1994) provide many examples of how we can work in our communities to improve community life in a participatory democratic way. They recommend that citizens gain greater influence over the media and become more active in local affairs. I also have previously mentioned the work of Kretzmann and McKnight (1993). Their asset-model of community development provides a comprehensive set of suggestions as to how to build upon individual and neighborhood assets to improve community life. I discuss an example of the community-asset model in relation to service learning in the next chapter.

I have focused somewhat on work and democracy, because I believe that any attempt to revitalize local participatory democracy must include these kinds of economic efforts. Without these efforts, I do not believe that we shall make much progress in the strengthening of strong democracy.

Having said this, I would be remiss if I did not acknowledge that strong democracy requires much more than promoting community economic development. We must attend to the celebration of local community, encourage local civic deliberation whenever possible, and recreate and strengthen our sense of the public. Briand (In press) provides a very thoughtful discussion of how to effectively conduct public forums. I discuss some of Briand's notions in the following chapter. Also, Boyte and Kari's (1996) discussion of the importance of public work underscores the importance a creating a sense of the public.

CIVIC LITERACY AND STRONG DEMOCRACY

We come to he heart of the issue here. I hope that I have made a case for the value of strong democracy, the commonwealth tradition, or civic republicanism. Promoting greater participatory democracy involves fostering the civic competence needed to sustain this form of democracy. Certainly education has a role; however, I would not want to repeat the mistake of philosophical liberal approaches to civic competence by maintaining that formal education is the sole repository for the development of civic consciousness. Nevertheless, education is critical to the development of civic competence. I discuss the educational role, particularly with respect to service learning in the final section of this book. For now we need to identify some of the competencies necessary for participatory democracy to achieve effectiveness.

Pratte (1988a) draws a distinction between "absolute" and "relative civic competence." A participatory form of democracy requires that political experts and professionals understand the intricacies of laws and statutes and the government infrastructure. However, we should close or narrow the gap in our society between the level of competence of our experts and those of ordinary citizens. Citizens need to develop what Pratte calls "relative competence."[3] Ordinary citizens must acquire the civic skills necessary for an effective participatory democracy. Citizens must understand how our form of government functions and their role as voters. But more yet is needed.

Pratte claims that first, and foremost, we must form a "civic conscience" among individuals. And I completely agree. Here civic republicanism reveals its value in contrast to procedural republicanism. The latter view, with its social contract undertow, assumes that individuals are primarily self-interested and sets as its civic task providing forms of civic education that will convince individuals that it is in their mutual self-interest to uphold moral norms.   As I have previously indicated, procedural republican approaches to moral and civic education mainly promote the value of cultivating a strong sense of freedom of choice, believing that morality requires this as the central individual value, along with justice. Individuals operating from the enlightened self-interest perspective obviously embrace the value of individual autonomy. The notion of the right (liberty and justice) eclipses the concept of the good of all or the common good.

In contrast, the civic republican point of view, as I have claimed, maintains that the common good should take primacy over "rights." I have added the rider that the only tenable concept of common good is one that includes securing the appropriate freedom and fairness essential for a good society.   And, of course, the democratic process must warrant specific liberties and procedures of fairness.

Assuming the civic republican view, then strong democracy requires the promotion of a civic conscience that adopts what I call the moral point of view, namely the recognition that we must base our decisions on a consideration of what promotes the best interests of all concerned, that is, the good of all. And it is here where moral education and the development of a civic conscience converge. Of course, the promotion of a civic conscience requires more than habits of decision making in terms of the moral point of view. It requires a willingness to respect the need of a public. We must develop "democratic selves," to adopt a phrase of Lappé and Du Bois (1994).

First, a democratic self should acknowledge one's self-interest in collective decisions. Being a democratically minded person does not mean being "selfless." We all have a self-interest at stake in public deliberation and achieving economically sustainable democratic communities. However, strong community cannot be achieved without basing our decisions on mutual commitment to the common good. And in some cases, the common good overrides individual self-interest. For example, a realtor may stand to earn a great deal of money by selling lots on the edge of town if the space is not converted to a green belt. But it may, indeed, be in the best interests of the community to use that land for a green belt.

Second, a democratic self is a person who has a fundamental sense of the public. Writers such as Palmer (1996) and Boyte and Kari (1996) discuss the importance of individuals seeing themselves as part of a public. Seeing oneself as a part of a public involves recognizing that we must secure the common good in our fundamental decisions and actions. This is central to the very notion of what it is to be a moral being or adopting the moral point of view (Lisman, 1996). Adopting the moral point of view is to base moral decisions on a consideration of what is in the best interests of all concerned. A central differences between the concern for the common good characteristic of the moral point of view and that of the democratic self is the difference between an inclination to base moral decisions on a consideration of what serves the interest of the good and a desire to contribution to the development of a society that nourishes the social sources of individual self-development. For example, we need to nourish those public spaces where community groups come together to deliberate and work together in the improvement of community life. We need to recognize that we must come together as a public to achieve many of our common goals. Palmer (1996) claims that "public life is ultimately grounded in an inward, spiritual sense of our relatedness to strangers" (p. 49).

Boyte and Kari (1996) stress the importance of our commitment to public work itself to the creation of commonwealth. They state:

The idea of public work offers a different strategy for overcoming divisions among diverse groups of Americans than what is conventionally used by those who call for harmony and renewal of community spirit. Public work allows groups to put aside divisions for the sake of combined effort toward common ends. We can recognize the need to work with others whom we do not like, whom we do not agree with, and whom we see as far different than those in our own community when there are larger public purposes. (p. 28)

The authors point out that public life contains pragmatic, problem-solving dimensions that bring together people with different conceptions of what is just and right (p. 28). Public life places a priority on taking action to alleviate problems or improve community life. "Public work teaches a different, richer, more complex view of 'truth'" (p. 29). It produces a collective wisdom and judgment instead of individual opinion. Boyte and Kari point out many historical examples of public work, such as the Civilian Conservation Corps in the New Deal. They state that public work is emerging in many settings, such as health care, higher education, approaches to youth development, and within professions such as journalism (p. 10). They emphasize that public work represents a fundamentally different way of understanding work. "Expertise becomes something that is part of a larger citizen effort, not the solution to problems" (p. 30). Public work promotes a citizen understanding of oneself as producer, instead of consumer.

Beyond developing a civic conscience or sense of democratic self, certain civic skills or competencies are also essential to support and strengthen participatory democracy. Briand (In press) highlights a number of participatory decision-making "skills" that democratic selves require. In Briand's terms, we need to be inclusive, comprehensive, deliberative, and cooperative. To be inclusive means to respect the diversity of others, to include others and respect the interests of everyone affected by our decisions. Comprehensive means to be "mutually comprehensive," that is, we should engage in reciprocal understanding, to attempt to understand and appreciate the perspectives of those with whom we deal. To be deliberative means that we are willing to engage in critical enquiry and deliberate with others in a spirit of mutual benefit.[4]

Recognizing that the kinds of decisions required are group decisions constitutes one of the most important competencies. Group decision making is not group think. Rather, this is a habit of mind that looks to the power of group decision making as one of the best ways to arrive at the best decision. Wallace (In press) observes that a distinguishing characteristic of Myles Horton's work at the Highlander Folk School was Horton's endorsement of group learning. Horton considered group learning superior to individual learning as a means of addressing community problems. Clearly, even in a community decision making setting, individuals should recognize when they need to withdraw and reflect carefully as an individuals. But, equally, we must be willing to engage in the kind of reciprocal trust in our fellow community members necessary to permit the group to arrive at the necessary decision.

Related to the skills of civic deliberation, Pratte (1988a) emphasizes the importance of developing a strong capacity for critical judgment and reflection. According to Pratte, reflective thinking is, in fact, principled thinking. "Judging according to principles entails judging non-arbitrarily, impartially, and objectively" (p. 173). Possessing a critical attitude is not merely having an ability to judge impartially, but recognizing a obligation to so judge, even when impartial judgment is not in one's self-interest (p. 174). Pratte observes:

Rather than cultivating the critical attitude that reflective thinking demands, some students cultivate a kind of nonreflective disposition that means leading narrow, restricted and privatized lives ruled over by an arbitrary particularity of the moment. It is the task of the teacher to help them understand that, in making such a decision, they are, in their existential ways, creating themselves and community, for there is a crucial relationship of mutual reciprocity between the community and its members. (p. 174)

Cultivating an ability to engage in structural analysis—getting at the roots of the problem—is a component of critical inquiry required for cultivating strong democracy. This kind of critical inquiry includes the ability to struggle against the tendency of bad faith—failing to acknowledge our class position in society—and remaining alert to hegemonic influences, that is, the pervasive influence of the values of the dominant class. The media constantly bombards us with hegemonic values, as I suggested in Chapter 6.

Gorham (1992) suggests that one way that we can counteract the tendencies of hegemony is to develop habits of countersocialization and reflective skepticism. Countersocialization is a habit of mind that consciously consider the widest diversity of opinions of important issues. This also involves reading texts with an attitude of persistent questioning. For example, in reading history, one should be alert to the value perspective of the historian. It is appropriate to asks, whose self-interest is served by the way historical events are constructed or narrated. Related to this approach is reflective skepticism, a form of thinking that consciously works at suspending assent until a thorough review of alternative perspectives has been considered. Instead of leaping to an endorsement of a view that is compatible with one's ideology, one should try to remain open to alternative perspectives.

One could add to Gorham's list the habit of "deconstruction," a willingness to understand how points of view, public opinion, community discussion, and other forms of narrative discourse are socially constructed in ways that serve vested interests. For example, feminist post-modernism, and related perspectives have contributed to our understanding of how women's self-understanding and view of society is socially constructed from the perspective male hegemony (Harvey, In press). In terms of developing a sense of the public, we need to deconstruct our excessive individualist assumptions about social policy, such as poverty and the nature and function of the political economy.

More broadly, we need to question our own individual ideological perspective. I have written about the complexities of this (Lisman, In press). A personal ideology is an individual's set of interrelated beliefs in which one's self-esteem is highly involved. Our ideological perspectives are not just constituted by a set of intellectual beliefs that are subject to the normal routines of confirmation and discomfirmation. Our ideology is fundamentally constituted by a set of emotionally relevant beliefs in which we interpret the significance of our experiences in highly self-involved ways. Many times our ideologies cloud our ability to assent to intellectual beliefs. For example, through reading sociological analysis, a person may see the point of a structural analysis of poverty, that is, poverty is caused by environmental factors, such as a lack of jobs that pay a meaningful wage, instead of being caused by the character flaws of the poor. However, because of the fact that this sociological analysis threatens a person's sense of self-esteem, or how the person tends to perceive the significance of the experience, the individual is reluctant to assent to the force of intellectual argument and sociological analysis. For example, perhaps an affluent individual through a structural understanding of poverty begins to feel guilty for his or her attempt to remain personally and socially distant from the plight of the poor. It is at this point where I think that service-leaning experiences can have an important effect in helping the individual overcome this kind of irrational disconnection between his or her emotional life (or set of self-involved appraisals or emotionally relevant beliefs) and set of intellectual beliefs..

Suffice it to say, that in order for us to begin as a society to achieve a more meaningful form of participatory democracy, it is important that through families, the community, and in formal education, we strive to educate ourselves and our young in ways that help promote the kind of civic competency necessary to sustain participatory democracy. These skills are not mastered at an early age, but, in fact, take a lifetime. And because our tendency to hubris, or pride, is always present, we must guard against personal frustration and moments in which we want to subvert the participatory decision making process through walking away from difficult decisions or by insisting on having our way. But, as Dewey, championed, I believe we can develop habits of democratic decision making that will enable us to work well in arriving at thoughtful group-based decisions that serve the common good.

STRONG DEMOCRACY, EDUCATION, AND SERVICE LEARNING

Having outlined a vision of what I think needs to happen to help bring about direct democracy and the civic competence that are necessary for us to develop and strengthen participatory democracy, education has a significant role in promoting the developing of the civic competencies of strong democracy. It has a role in first in relation to student development and in terms of campus and community partnerships.

Student Development

I outlined the civic virtues or civic competencies that are essential for the development of strong democracy. These include a civic conscience, a willingness to engage in participatory decision making, and persistent critical inquiry. It is important that educators model these values in their teaching.

In the first place, educators need to work to change their conception of public policy stemming from professional or expert management to that of relative civic competence. Teachers and professors need to see themselves not as dispensers of knowledge and expertise, which only reinforces the gap between absolute and relative civic competence. To this end, educators must critique the pretensions of scientism and instrumental reason.

Educators also need to help empower students to understand the important role they can play within a democracy. Civic skills need to be modeled and practiced in the classroom itself. Bricker (1989) has advocated that cooperative learning can help develop democratic skills. But I believe we must go beyond this. Students should be given many options, and as much as possible they should have the opportunity to decide on a democratic basis what community projects to support. Students may move in directions that a faculty member might not prefer. However, unless there are other significant overriding factors, faculty members should not interfere except in his or her role to ensure that the service projects are academically relevant. An example of an be overriding factor might be one of a student wanting to try to impose a project upon a community group. The student, let us suppose, fails to develop a proposed project in consultation with the community. This violates one of the most important principles of good service learning in the community, as I shall discuss in Chapter 9. In that case, the faculty member must insist that students not only practice democratic decision making within the classroom, but support the demo-cratic process out in the community among the citizens with whom they work.

Students and faculty are not equals. The faculty member has a responsibility to provide guidance and knowledge, and, indeed, students expect this. In particular, a faculty member is obliged to bring his or her scholarly expertise to bear on an issue. If, for example, students in a science class proposed a scientifically or environmental unworkable plan in the community, the science, the professor must point out the limitations of the project. The professor certainly is within his or her rights to overrule the project if it is without scientific merit.

The other issue that bears touching upon is that of the alleged procedural liberalism of the classroom. I mentioned that the justice model of service learning has been criticized on these grounds. For example, a professor committed to having students work toward social transformation, may direct students toward activities counter to their sensibilities. Some students may not want to work for greater social justice.

Justice-oriented faculty, and maybe even some students, may regard this kind of civic community-development model I am advocating as "conservative," or as not really "getting into justice issues." And, I must confess, there is some merit to this criticism. This criticism is not unrelated to Boyte and Farr's (1997) claim that the volunteerist mode of service learning advocates service as a way to promote an ethic of service—in order to help people feel more communal and kindly toward one another. I have criticized this perspective as well.

A danger exists, that the civic literacy model may be content with helping community members feel better about each other and more trustful. However, from the strong democracy or civic republican perspective, developing a caring and trustful attitude among others in one's community does not suffice. This merely begins a process of working together in a community toward creating a strong democratic, deliberative process leading to the improvement of community life and the strengthening of the democratic process, including economic democracy. Stopping short of these objectives does a great disservice to the strong democracy model.

Another concern, often reflected among more radical justice advocates, particularly among the neo-Marxists, has to do with the fact of hegemony—the bad faith perspective of students and community members. We must be on guard against a tendency of students and community members alike to do shallow rather than deep community work. Shallow work is mainly cosmetic, such as cleaning up the community or simply promoting more socializing. Indeed, as I suggest elsewhere, such activities may be the first step of community development. But it is only the starting point in creating sustainable democratic communities

This issue can occur in community development; for example, if a college group works with a low-income neighborhood group in a community beautification project. Neighborhood members may feel happier because their community looks nicer, and the students may feel happier because they have a tangible result of some hard work they have put into the community. One outstanding problem exists. The community members remain in poverty, and still, let us suppose, underemployed or unemployed. These issues must be addressed. It may be that a class project must be limited to community beautification. However, the service-learning program at the college or the university must be prepared to work further and deeper with this community, if educational institution commits to a commonwealth or community development model of service learning. Those who continue to interact with the community must help the community members broaden their thinking about what they might be able to do democratically to address their more severe economic needs. The community and the institution of higher education need to begin to consider how they might promote community economic development. Academically-based community service, unfortunately, may tend to define community problems in ways that match the needs and capacities of the university. But these may not be the needs of the community. If the college or university cannot take this next step, then they should consider stepping out of the picture and find someone who can. Community building of the shallow sort is more about do-goodism than it is about empowering community members to seek and find solutions to their deepest concerns and problems.

When done in the spirit of strong democracy, addressing these deeper, admittedly controversial pedagogical and community issues is an improvement over the justice approach in at least two ways. In the first place justice issues are worked on in the context of community development. To their credit, justice advocates contend that their interests lie in social transformation, which requires addressing the structural problems. Crime and drug abuse must be prevented. But the root causes of poverty must be attacked if our society is effectively to reduce crime and drug abuse. Of course, I have pointed out that justice advocates tend to adopt a single-issue approach to community work, neglecting the organic nature of communities and the interconnection of a whole host of complex social issues, such as poverty, racism, crime, gang violence, poor school achievement, and environmental degradation.

Professorial justice advocates also tend to address justice issues in the abstract through classroom lecture and writing articles and books. This kind of professional detachment from concrete, local issues produces unrealistic solutions. Students become worked up over issues with no way to address them. By grounding justice work in the democratic experience of deliberation and action through a consultation process involving, first and foremost, the community members, one can rest assured that decisions will not be carried out in the abstract. It is better to get rid of one slum lord than to issue an academic manifesto against slumlords. The civic approach sees that these issues must be approached in a holistic way; for they all are connected to democratic and economic disenfranchisement in local communities.

Although we would like to have a national impact, I am firmly convinced that this can only be achieved through helping local communities become more democratic and economically secure. Locally empowered citizens will then begin to find their common political purpose, which then will have a national impact.

Elitist perspectives also have criticized this focus of the civic model on local communities. According to Rimmerman (1997a), elitists claim that the participatory model is unrealistic. Widespread decision making is not feasible in a society of more than two hundred fifty million people (p. 24). Elitists also contend that populists have an exaggerated sense of the capabilities of ordinary citizens to engage in civic deliberation. Critics fear that encouraging greater public decision making will destabilize the communities and the workplace. Further, increased citizen participation "replaces clear legislative goals and fosters fragmentation throughout the policymaking and implementation process" (p. 25).

However, if we think of increased civic participation in terms of local community development, many of these concerns are not justified. Citizens can acquire the skills they need to make effective decisions concerning their local communities. And rather than clouding the legislative process, stronger civic communities will ensure than their elected representatives are representing deep community needs and interests, rather than, which is all to often, the interests of the affluent class. Moreover, instead of contributing to political instability, greater participatory democracy can counteract, what I believe to be the greatest threats to democracy we currently face—civic apathy, misplaced anti-federalism, and cultural and political hegemony. Finally, it is through members of sustainable democratic communities finding common voice in addressing local, state, regional, and national issues, through appropriate venues, including electoral, that a society of millions can be democratically effective.

I mentioned that one of the biggest challenges to a more participatory form of decision making is the fact that people become stuck within their own ideologies, their highly self-involved ways of experiencing the significance of the world, their emotionally relevant beliefs. I believe that service learning can become a powerful way for positioning students to experience the world in ways that draw them out of their ideological stances. As students become acquainted with homeless individuals or poor children in the schools, they can began to sense the humanity of those whom they serve and begin to create a greater sense of solidarity. Through processes such as this, students and others can begin to alter their set of ideological beliefs and become receptive to rational evidence. Their intellectual beliefs and emotionally relevant beliefs begin to converge.

In conclusion, I want to emphasize that the form of education required by a civic republican approach is not just a "civic education," or an education in how the government works. As I have mentioned, Harkavy (August, 1996) has criticized Barber (1992) for relying to heavily on formal civic education—even though informed by service learning—as the catalyst for social transformation.   Rather, this civic literacy promotes civic conscience and a sense of the democratic self. It also involves developing habits of persistent critical inquiry in which students and others are willing to question the underlying hegemonic assumptions of our society and willing to work in participatory democratic community in developing efforts to help improve community life and developing sustainable democratic communities. This form of education requires an approach to service learning that moves beyond volunteerism and experiential education. Volunteerism, as I have previously argued, tends to reinforce a privatistic approach to social analysis and the social dependency that comes with mere charity. Experiential education reinforces scientism and instrumental reason through neglecting to assist students in understanding the moral dimensions of academic disciplines and by reinforcing an expert consumerist view of democracy.

A community-development approach to service learning is required for cultivating the civic skills required for strong democracy. Again, this is a form of service in which students arrive at projects through a participatory decision making process that begins in the classroom. But this effort extends into the community, where students work alongside community members, learning from those members as they work in mutually supportive ways to help improve community life and strengthen participatory democratic decision making within the community.

It would be naive, to fail to recognize that economic inequity is at the heart of many of our community issues. Although much community work can take place in a political non-confrontational way, as Kretzmann and McKnight (1993) illustrate. Nevertheless, students and community members can not always avoid confrontation with those whose vested interests are counter to the community-based interests of the have nots. Students and community members will discover they must struggle for their rights. Confrontational tactics may have to be adopted. But if confrontation is necessary, community members will more likely succeed through a community development model. By creating a greater sense of community and by developing a civic conscience and critical thinking skills, and through having achieved some improvement in their community life, community members will be much more able effective in their confrontational efforts.

One must keep ever present, the overarching goal of working to build economically sustainable democratic communities. And the educator must also keep this in mind as he or she helps students understand the ways in which their academic work can be made relevant to the community needs. Students can utilize action research and group problem solving as they attempt to bring educational resources to bear on addressing community problems and working with community members to help improve community life. Through this process students and faculty can themselves benefit as much as the community is benefited. For educationally, this work constitutes the social construction of participatory democratic decision making, which involves strong collaboration between institutions of education and the community.

Campus and Community Partnerships

First, education must be good community partner, especially institutions of higher education. The service-learning movement is producing a recognition of the importance of strengthening campus and community partnerships. This clearly is a trend in the right direction. I shall say more about this effort in Chapter 9. Also, the service-learning movement itself can be a catalyst for creating and strengthening community relationships. But this must be an intentional effort. We should not expect our communities or our students to become more civically involved merely through sending students out into the community mainly to provide direct service in local community-based agencies and organizations. At best, as Rimmerman (1997b) has observed, students performing direct service may achieve a heightened sense of the importance of community involvement, which, of course, is a step in the right direction.

On the community side, one of the central concerns is with the fact that our social service agencies, as important as they are to providing the kinds of services needed in our challenged communities, all too often, as McKnight (1995) has observed create greater individual dependency on these services. This happens because of what McKnight calls a "need-based" approach or perspective. Individuals are perceived as having problems that the agencies can "correct" or address. Little encouragement is given to individuals to find solutions to their problems. Boyte (1991) contends that this kind of service approach to society fosters the therapeutic attitude toward the economically disadvantaged which is endemic to our society.

I have mentioned that civic skills can not be developed in a vacuum. This point can not be stated too strongly. I have insisted that this kind of civic literacy must be done in the context of community-based work—in fact, community development. Of course, many community development approaches exist, from Alinsky's (1971) to the Kretzmann and McKnight (1993) community-asset model. For the moment, I want to focus not so much on the product or the particular kind of community development activity, but the process. The process of community development must be one in which both students, faculty, and community members all find civic empowerment in activities aimed at improving community life. What would such activities look like?

There are certain principles of good practices regarding such campus and community partnerships, which I discuss in Chapter 9. For the moment, I want to emphasize that one can not get anywhere in a community without developing a basic level of trust between the campus partners and the members of the community. I have learned in the Community College of Aurora's college's community development efforts that one must proceed slowly and with a humble recognition that the college's agenda may not be the same as the community's. Securing trust between and among all participants is the first step of campus and community collaboration. For example, suppose a neighborhood group wants to develop a community garden. The first step, then, is for the college students and faculty to collaborate with the community group and to encourage the community members to take as much of a leadership role as possible. Service-learning students should work in a supportive role in which they never dictate to community members what should be done. The same applies to the university or college faculty member who may be working alongside the college students in the community. Later, once trust is established, the community members may begin to take on larger responsibilities, such as providing a neighborhood watch or even to begin to work on economic development or improved housing. I shall say more about some of these principles of good practice in Chapter 9.

NOTES

1. I noted in Chapter Two that the concept of "The New Citizenship" first occurs, as far as I can tell in *Civic Declaration: A Call for New Citizenship*.

2. In my discussion of Sandel, I draw mainly from his excellent summary of his book in *The Atlantic Monthly*. However, for the detailed historical account, the full book is well worth reading.

3. I am not happy with the term "relative competence" for the simple reason that it might be confused with ethical relativism. Clearly, Pratte is not an ethical relativist, however.

4. Briand has provided several formulations of these skills. My own adaptation, presented here, does not completely correspond with Briand. But I hope to present these skills in the spirit of Briand's work.

8

A Community-Development Approach to Service Learning

Before surveying some examples of best practices in community and campus partnerships, I want to list and briefly discuss some of the productive service strategies that may be required by a community-development model of service learning, which I consider to be the civic model. I provide only a sampling and I know that many others will surface as we grow in this effort. Please bear in mind that some of this material is repeated elsewhere in this book.

CLASSROOM PRACTICES

Classes should be taught as democratically as possible. Students should have a democratic student voice in the decisions as to what kind of projects the class should be involved in. This recognizes procedural liberalism in the classroom, that is assuring consideration of all relevant points of view on issues. Also, if some students object to participating in those projects that the class decides upon democratically, the professor should give other service alternatives.

Self-Empowerment

We all have a self-interest at stake in community work and development. We can grow as individuals through this kind of work, through improving old skills and developing new ones. And we can gain a greater sense of self-esteem and personal assurance as we become more strongly connected with others in the community.

In order to prepare students for this kind of work, then, it is appropriate to help students focus on their own needs and abilities. One can utilize some kind of a version of the personal asset inventory of Kretzmann and McKnight (1993) in which students are asked to provide self-inventories regarding the assets they bring to community work. Students could be asked to identify specific skills they posses in areas such as health, office, construction and repair, transportation, and child care, to name a few examples. Students also could be asked to identify what three things they do best and if there are any skills they would like to teach.

Or as *By the people* (1995) recommends, students can be encouraged simply to tell their own stories. Examples of questions that students may be asked to write about or discuss are: "What is the most frightening thing that ever happened to you? Who is the most unusual person you ever met? What is your greatest learning experience? Who is the person you will never forgive? and Who is the most influential person in your life?" (p. 11). These kinds of discussions help us better understand who we are and what we care the most about. They help us identify our talents and interests and prepare us to draw upon our personal values and commitments as we engage in public life.

Group Problem Solving

Yelsma (1994) advocates small group problem solving in service-learning courses. This approach, of course, is not limited to a community-development approach to service learning, but it is useful in classroom and service-learning practice. Yelsma emphasizes the importance of having students learn group problem-solving techniques through service learning. He illustrates this with an example of students working with unmarried, pregnant high school women. Yelsma found that as students worked together as a group on this project, engaging in appropriate research and working with the women in the community, they focused on practicing good communication techniques within the group.

As with all group communication, the kind of communication principles advocated by Briand (In press), which I discussed in the previous chapter, such as deliberation, inclusion, and comprehension become vital. Students should respect each others' divergent points of view. They should put themselves in the shoes of their opponents and those whom they serve as much as possible. They also need to understand that by engaging in community-development work they are engaging in public work. Students need opportunities to reflect on the nature of public work and how it differs from individual effort. And most important, they need to find consensus, or at least a workable middle-ground if they are to move together on an issue.

Class-based group projects are useful to make progress in community-development service learning. Developing class-based community projects in a democratic way prepares students to work democratically in the community. If students mainly go off as individuals to do service-learning projects, chances are they will mainly be doing direct service on the volunteer model. Consequently, they will not be thrust into a group decision-making process in which they could practice the principles of democratic decision making and communication. Second, the professor should foster the value of group decision making itself over individual decision making. This can only be carried out in the classroom through group problem solving and action, and it can only be deployed in service as students work in groups on community-based projects; hence, the importance of group problem solving techniques.

These principles apply equally in the context of working with community groups in a campus and community partnership. Trust must be established through reliability and respect. And as the campus and community group begin to deliberate together about possible community projects, these principles of community decision making and communication must be adhered to.

ENGAGING WITH THE COMMUNITY

As I suggest in the following chapter, working through specific mediating institutions or local associations is one of the best ways for a class or an educational institution achieve community impact. Examples of such community-based organizations are community schools, family centers, ethnic associations, church groups, neighborhood associations, or non-profit community economic development organizations. Building trust between the campus representatives—students and professors and the community-based organization—as I have stated several times, is the most basic principle of this kind of community development work. I have learned from experience that educational partner can do a great deal of damage by approaching the community with an attitude of having all the answers to the community's problems. This reeks of elitism. And it also violates one of the fundamental principles of community work: do not do for others what they must do for themselves.

But how do you approach a community-based organization? Below are several strategies that not only provide avenues to the community but also provide concrete things that one can do to make something happen. As a preface to this, one needs to be sensitive to how community members relate to one another. As a first step, I would recommend visiting a community organization several times before ever doing anything. Simply ask if you may come as a friendly observer. Explain that you are trying to understand how people work together in the community, and ask if you can sit in on a board meeting or in a community meeting. Be friendly and observe silently. You will quickly learn the importance of observing informal protocols that must be observed. Some ethnic groups like to begin with friendly conversation or a meal. In fact, when you begin to work with a community organization, you may discover that you need to establish trust and familiarity through informal gatherings over a period of time before you can "get down to business." Assuming that you have established the requisite trust and basis for acceptance, then there are a number of possible strategies that the class or college group can use.

Determining Others' Self-Interests

As *By the People* (1995), suggests, it is important to engage in a public discussion with community group members to determine their self-interests. Small focus groups probably work best for this. Questions should be more public than personal. While community members may tell powerful and personal stories to dramatize their needs and interests, the discovery process should be focused on learning what the individuals want from their group and their community. This effort is about helping individuals work more effectively together in improving community life. So the questions should be focused on what individuals want for themselves and for their community through their group activities. You could ask members questions such as, "Why do you belong to this group?" "What do you want from your group?" "What personal interests attract you to this group?" "What do you really like about this group?" "What concerns do you have about this group?"

These focus group questions and answers can become the basis for beginning to frame the kinds of discussion and action plans one might wish to bring to the larger group. It is important that you have the group's permission to bring this discovery to the larger group. And, in fact, it is probably best to have members from the community report back to the group.

Interviewing for Information

In some cases, the campus side of the partnership may be invited into a group. A need may already have been identified. Perhaps a group is concerned about crime in the neighborhood, and they have invited a criminal justice professor and a group of students to a community meeting to help the neighborhood group brainstorm about what steps can be taking to address their problem. It is important in this case that a careful effort be made to obtain information. After hearing some of the concerns from the plenary group, everyone should break out into smaller groups to get information on the problems being confronted. A list should be kept of the kind of outside information that must be collected, in this case—what the city police are already doing in the neighborhood to counteract crime, whether there is a neighborhood watch organization, and similar data. Follow-up interviews to the outside authorities or sources of information will need to be made. And this, of course, will be an excellent activity for students. Community members should be encouraged to participate in acquiring this information. They must be included in every step of the process.

Taking Civic Inventories

As background work to becoming involved with a specific group, it may be important from the perspective of the campus partnership to take a civic inventory of one's local community. What important associations exist? What do they do in the community? Who are the important individuals in the community who tend to make things happen? Who are the vocal community critics? Who are those most likely to engage in blocking techniques? Finding answers to these and related questions contributes to progress in community work. The community group may discover that they need to gain a better understanding of the community from this perspective. Again, students, faculty, and community members can divide up the tasks and began to take such a civic inventory.

Doing Community-Asset Inventories

As I discuss in the next chapter, one of the most powerful ways to gain entry into a community is through community-asset inventories. Kretzmann and McKnight (1993) discuss this strategy at length. Students and even other community members sometimes need to go door-to-door in a community and find out the gifts and talents that individuals have to share with the community. This can be a procedure for determining a possible economic development initiative. Perhaps the community already has decided that it wants to create more jobs through developing microenterprise or home-based business initiatives. One of the useful tasks may be to canvass the neighborhood to learn what kind of talents and interests people have which could be converted to small businesses. Kretzmann and McKnight tell a story of how a soul-food business started in a Chicago housing project by just this means.

This approach also can be taken in trying to strengthen a neighborhood association or another community-based organization. Perhaps the organization needs more members. By going door-to-door and doing an asset-inventory, one can identify potential talents and interests that individuals can bring to a community organization and begin to strengthen the organization by recruiting these members.

Mapping Power

As I have previously stated, community power issues are omnipresent within low-income communities. But sometimes, the perceived power is not identical to the real power. Neighborhood groups must understand this point. As I have mentioned earlier a false assumption that the people have no power and that the real power rests with elected officials is a major cause of our civic distemper. While legislative authority is the seat of much political power, the power to change things does not necessarily reside with legislative power. Obtaining a sense of where the power is within the community enriches community development.

Developing a power map involves identifying a particular issue of concern, such as community beautification. After identifying some of the problem sites, such as vacant lots, alleys, and graffiti sites, one might began to determine the limiting factors or barriers or obstacles to getting things done. The existence of a gang, or an absentee owner of a vacant lot or building may be obstacles. Or the community may lack of sense of pride. The group then should identify interests and resources for addressing these issues. Perhaps a local church could promote community pride, or the community could host a "pride day" with a parade. Or an important city council person can obtain neighborhood improvement funds. The result of such mapping will be to give the campus and community members with a better understanding of how to proceed.

Also one may want to know more about the power structure of the community group one plans to work with. Students may engage in focus group or small group discussions in which questions such as these are asked, "What kind of power do the people you want to work with have? How can you work with them? Does the organization work well the way the power is structured? What do you notice about the informal power relationships?" (*By the people*, p. 32).

Providing a Structural Analysis

Helping community-based organizations arrive at a structural analysis of problems is at the heart of participatory democratic action. Due to the operation of hegemony in our society, we are constantly side-tracked from focusing on the most basic aspect of our community problems. Community groups are very susceptible to this. Community groups often organize around immediate concerns such as crime or a need for neighborhood beautification. This may be a first step toward community development work. From the campus side of the equation, we will never accomplish anything if we fail to meet community members on their own grounds and work with them on their issues. But the kinds of mediating agencies I have mentioned, such as neighborhood organizations, family centers, and community schools are important places where the community members and the college members can gather to address community concerns and issues.

Chris Berkowitz of the Aurora Project in Aurora, Colorado, an umbrella "healthy communities" nonprofit organization, likes to get community members as quickly as possible to begin to see problems in a more structural way. Berkowitz uses the analogy of a flower, suggesting that the petals are the "presenting issues," the stem the "supporting issues," and the root the "root cause." This can be a useful activity to help community members, when the time is ripe, to move deeper into community issues. For example, perhaps the higher education representatives and the community members have concluded a successful community beautification project. Vacant lots and alleys have been cleaned up; a vacant house has received a new coat of paint; graffiti has been removed from several buildings. But gangs still persist in the neighborhood; many people are unemployed or underemployed, children have nowhere to go after school. These issues need to be addressed. Building upon the success of the beautification project and using an activity such as the flower example, perhaps the group could begin to see the previously deteriorated condition of the neighborhood and the graffiti as presenting issues. Supporting issues are crime and gangs and underemployment. The root cause of lack of jobs and economic inequality begins to surface as an item of discussion. The group then might be ready to proceed to discuss issues such as how to engage in community economic development.

Community Problem Solving and Community Self-Leadership

These steps and strategies I have discussed above, are part of a community problem solving. Often the academic side discusses this kind of activity in terms of action-research, the effort of engaging in academic research to help solve community problems (Wals et al., 1990). Although Wals and associates discuss this approach in the context of environmental work and more in relation to students than community members, I think this is a powerful concept suitable for appropriate community-development. Action research can be a process in which faculty and student are doing most of the work. And if done this way, this research may create the impression that the community is simply being used as a laboratory for university research. But as Wals and associates point out the community members should be involved in this kind of research whenever possible. Having community members not only involved in defining the problems and issues to be addressed but contributing to the research in the community can be a galvanizing experience for community members. This approach also will allay the suspicion that the college is using the community as an academic laboratory. Alanah Fitch, a chemistry professor at Loyola University Chicago involves her undergraduate and graduate students, as well as middle school children in conducting lead testing. Community organizations are using this information to pinpoint the source of lead poisoning among children in city neighborhoods (Fitch, 1997). Janet Smith, a student in the Ph. D. Program of Urban Studies at Cleveland State University, and Bobbie Reichtell, a Housing Development Specialist for the Broadway Area Housing Coalition (Smith and Reichtell, 1997) collaborated in a research effort regarding fair housing. Their research involved community members, and in fact led to a decision to continue working on housing issues, but to develop a process to facilitate community building.

The most important point for community problem solving is to keep in mind that this approach involves group decision making. One must work in and through the community as a group in order to identity the community problem, to understand barriers and resources, and to develop an action plan and eventually to act. To repeat, Myles Horton, founder of the Highlander Folk School, believed that group problem solving is more powerful than individual problem solving. This does not mean that individuals within a group can not make individual contributions and suggestions. But the effort must be collective.

The higher education members in a campus and community partnership can play an important role in this. Sometimes students have greater leisure to do some of the community research necessary to developing an action plan. In a well organized community-development service-learning course, the professor may be able to devise ways that students can learn academic skills and knowledge in working on such a project. However, as I have stressed several times, the higher education side of the partnership should not try to structure the problem in ways that play to their strength. The community may not want or need what the college has to offer. One should realize when one's services are not needed.

I find that I must constantly guard against the temptation of trying to get people to where I want them to be before they are ready. Being anxious for community members to see the structural problems, I am always tempted to provide the analysis for them. But this alienates the community members. The community members (and the students for that matter) will come to a structural understanding when they are ready. College resources also must be judiciously offered. A professor may have useful resource for a community organization—perhaps the professor and the students are skilled at statistic analysis. But community members need to discover their own resources. Building community members group problem solving capacity is as important as solving the problem.

I might add that, as Horton believed, facilitating group problem solving is one of the most important role of an educator in community work. The educator should not regard himself or herself as the knowledge expert. Facilitating group problem solving is essential for participatory democracy in the service of building sustainable democratic communities. Individually led efforts may accomplish something important in the short run. But unless the community members have been empowered to be the problem solvers themselves, once the important leader is gone, the community group is usually back at square one. This is why I advocate what Briand (In press) calls "community self-leadership."

Confrontational Politics

At the present moment community-asset development is in vogue. It is a very useful approach to community work. But it also is popular because it is a "low grade" method of confrontation, especially when compared to the work of Alinsky (1971). But we must remember that confrontational politics is useful and necessary. Perhaps a neighborhood group feels that unless an absentee landlord cleans and boards up a particular house, it will continue to be used as a crack house. Confrontational techniques may be necessary to get the absentee landlord to do something about his vacant house. The community group may want to take out an advertisement in the local newspaper and list the number of rundown properties this particular landlord has or bring his name before the city council. Regardless of the tactic, confrontation at times is fundamentally necessary. One can not do better than to consult Alinsky to acquire these kinds of political tools.

We must recognize that the most fundamental task in promoting strong participatory democracy is to build strong, sustainable democratic communities. The campus can be a strong partner with local communities. And as I have said repeatedly, building trust and reciprocity is the first step of strong campus and community collaboration. Empowering community members to work through the democratic process to improve community life is equally important. Certainly, professors and students can be powerful allies in this community endeavor. Professors and students can provide important and necessary community research. The college can bring job training and small business development training to local communities. The small business arm of the college can help a community nonprofit organization develop a for-profit business. But at every step of the way, community members must be vitally involved and must develop their own capacity to improve community life.

9

Principles and Best Practices of Campus and Community Partnerships

In this chapter, I briefly discuss some emerging principles of best practices concerning campus and community partnerships. I then discuss examples of some efforts in Pennsylvania, Minnesota, and Colorado that exemplify programs based on these principles. These principles do not discuss service learning. But since this book is partly about service learning, I have selected projects that incorporate some version of this pedagogy. In the final chapter, I attempt to pull together the threads of where we are in higher education at the present moment and suggest the direction in which higher education needs to move, a direction consistent with these principles and practices and in line with the commonwealth or civic republican view of academically based community service and civic literacy. A historian might argue that this chapter should be put in the historical context. I attempt that in the final chapter.

THE WINGSPREAD PRINCIPLES OF BEST PRACTICES FOR CAMPUS AND COMMUNITY PARTNERSHIPS[1]

In the summer of 1997, a Wingspread conference at the Johnson Foundation in Racine, Wisconsin, was convened to discuss some examples of community and higher education collaborations, many of which have been funded through the federal department of Housing and Urban Development (HUD) Campus and Community Partnership initiative.[2] Among those instrumental in organizing this meeting were Gib Robinson of

San Francisco University and Ira Harkavy of the University of Pennsylvania. I participated in the meeting on behalf of the American Association of Community Colleges. This was the second Wingspread conference on this subject.

The intensive weekend conference, which included participants from community-based organizations that have been working with colleges and universities, college and university representatives, foundation program officers, and representatives from the federal government, produced working guidelines for campus and community partnerships. As the phrase "working guidelines" suggest, these principles will be further refined. But I believe that the basic concepts undergirding strong campus and community collaboration have been captured. I have created a list of these principles.

- Partnerships should share a commitment to a shared vision, values, and goals. At the center of those goals is the creation of "sustainable democratic urban communities." To achieve that goal, the partnerships should develop and proceed through an ongoing democratic process and approaches which emphasize increasing the capacity and power of the local community and its members, helping to achieve genuine equality.
- Partnerships should share a basis of respect between and among the partners, as well as a respect and a commitment to the partnership.
- The partnership should be long-term, serious, and sustained, involving multiple sectors in deepening and broadening relationships.
- Partnerships should be based on mutual and common benefit and the need for change and improvement of all partners.
- Learning, research, and assessment of the partnership and its results should be on-going.
- Partnerships should be based on actions that involve concrete, real world success that lead to achieving sustainable urban communities.
- Partnerships should involve institutional structures that promote institutional change and ongoing innovation, as well as cooperation and collaboration among partners.

I will make some summative remarks about these principles, following a brief look at examples of "best practices." As I have already indicated from previous examples in this book, some very interesting work is occurring across the country involving campus and community partnerships embodying these types of principles. I can only present a snapshot of some of these practices. There are many more, but as I wanted to select some examples of these kinds of partnerships that involved service learning, I have limited myself to such examples.

BEST PRACTICES

University of Pennsylvania and West Philadelphia

In 1985, Ira Harkavy and Sheldon Hackney (before he became president of Penn) offered a history seminar entitled "Urban University-Community Relationships: Penn-West Philadelphia, Past, Present, and Future, as a Case Study." The purpose of this seminar was to focus on the problems of West Philadelphia in the context of thinking about the relevance and role of the university responding to community needs. Harkavy (Benson and Harkavy, 1991), in discussing the origins of this effort, noted that West Philadelphia was deteriorating. Harkavy and Hackney were interested in exploring such questions as, "What should Penn do to remedy its 'environmental situation'?" "Why study History? Knowledge for what?" and "What are universities good for?"

In the seminar, each student conducted research on a problem that was adversely affecting specific groups in West Philadelphia. Several students focused on the problem of youth unemployment. In response to this problem, these students proposed the development of a community-based, summer job-training program for at-risk youth. The West Philadelphia Improvement Corps (WEPIC) was created in the summer of 1985. This project focused on projects at Bryant School, a neighborhood elementary school. The youth removed graffiti, painted murals around the school building and a nearby day-care center, and improved the school grounds, planting trees, shrubs, grass, and ground cover, and constructing brick walks and benches.

Harkavy notes that, as the work proceeded, neighbors pitched in and helped and even undertook improvement projects on their own properties. Penn faculty and students realized that public schools might be able to serve as centers both for youth-work experiences and for neighborhood revitalization (p. 16). WEPIC became an extracurricular after-school program at Bryant. Harkavy adds:

From the Bryant elementary school, WEPIC spread over the next five years to a large comprehensive high school, three middle schools, and two other elementary schools. It is currently a year round school neighborhood revitalization program involving nearly a thousand students, their parents, and community members in education, cultural, recreation, job training and community improvement and service activities. (p. 16)

Since then, WEPIC is no longer administered by Penn. "The program is now administratively coordinated by the West Philadelphia Partnership, a mediating organization composed of West Philadelphia institutions (including Penn) and community groups, in conjunction with the Greater Philadelphia Urban Affairs Coalition and Philadelphia School District" (Benson and Harkavy, 1991, p.16).

While continuing to support the WEPIC activities, Harkavy has launched many other projects out of his Center for University and Community Partnerships and has emerged as a national leader on promoting university and campus partnerships. He continues to advocate the central role of community schools as viable mediating institutions for enabling institutions of higher education to partner effectively in the community.

In a more recent publication, Harkavy (1996, August) discusses several more recent community school efforts involving academically based community service. In this article, Harkavy critiques the service-learning movement for continuing to propagate mainly direct service (volunteerism). He writes:

Urban colleges and universities are in a unique position to go beyond service learning (and its inherent limitations) to strategic academically-based community service, which has as its primary goal contributing to the well-being of people in the community both in the here and now and in the future. It is service rooted in an intrinsically tend to teaching and research, and it aims to bring about *structural* community improvement (e.g., effective public schools, neighborhood economic development, strong community organizations) rather than simply to alleviate individual misery (e.g., feeding the hungry, sheltering the homeless, tutoring the "slow learner"). (p. 6)

Harkavy cites two Penn seminars that have focused on advancing community school development, Anthropology 210 and Sociology 302 (p.18). Anthropology 210, which emphasizes the relationships between anthropology and biomedical science, was created to link Penn's premedical training with the Anthropology Department's program in Medical Anthropology. Professor Francis Johnston, who teaches the seminar, decided to add an academically based community service component in which his students and he would work with the Turner Middle School in West Philadelphia in which more than 84% of the students come from low-income communities. At this time Turner Middle School was converting into a community-school—a school that provides a variety of community services at the school site.

From 1990 to date, the students in this anthropology course have "carried out a variety of activities at Turner focused on the interactive relationships among diet, nutrition, growth, and health" (p. 19). Harkavy adds: "Students are encouraged to view their education at Penn as preparing them to contribute to the solution of societal problems through service to the local community, and to do so by devoting a large part of their work in the course to a significant human problem, in this case the 'nutriture' of disadvantaged inner-city children" (p. 19). This endeavor has resulted in the creation of a "nutrition laboratory" in West Philadelphia at Turner.

A few years ago, Penn's Zellerbach Family Professor of Sociology and Research, Frank F. Furstenberg, Jr., began a "communal participatory action research project at University City High School" (p. 21). Nearly 90 % of its students came from low-income families, with 50% of its students receiving a D or an F in at least one course, and with a high drop-out rate. "Furstenberg was the first of approximately fifteen faculty to connect his or her academic work with University City High School" (p. 21).

Furstenberg's main effort has been to address, through his course, the issue of teen pregnancy. With the assistance of the undergraduates in his course, Furstenberg has been working on developing a teen pregnancy prevention program. Teams of students have collected baseline data on teen parents and demographics of the school population in general. The school principal and teachers are using this information to develop an effective teen pregnancy prevention program.

I recently visited two of the community middle schools in West Philadelphia, Turner, and Shaw. Joan Weeks, Associate Director of Penn Program for Public Services, arranged these visits and accompanied me. I experienced the power of the community school concept. I visited with Charles D'Alfonso, Principal of Turner, and Kathleen Lee, a language arts teacher. Turner borders a more upscale part of West Philadelphia but also serves students from the lower income parts of the area. Mr. D'Alfonso was very enthusiastic about the Middle School/Penn partnership.

Several unique features characterize these schools. First, as community schools, social workers provide support for family members. Turner has a Saturday program in which parents can take enrichment courses. A swimming pool and gymnasium are open. Community-based organizations hold meetings at the school. Shaw Middle School conducts a Wednesday evening community school. This program features a special tutoring class for students, a computer class open to community members, art classes, and a job readiness program in which a career counselor offers guidance and resources for employment.

Second, the Penn and community school partnership provides important educational opportunities. While Penn students and students from other universities provide tutoring assistance, the WEPIC Program, which is how the school staff refers to the Penn program, involves Penn students in a more substantial way in the classroom than merely tutoring. Penn students get to assist in class room instruction of topics they are studying at the university.

For example, currently at Turner, students in Francis Johnston's Anthropology 25-301, "Health in Urban Communities" develop curriculum and teach health topics to Turner Middle School students who, in turn, teach these health lessons to their peers. The course focuses on nutrition intervention to improve eating habits. A graduate student assistant to Francis Johnson, Penny Gordon-Larsen, teaches Anthropology 310-301, "Biomedical Science and Human Adaptability." Penn undergraduates teach and conduct research with the Turner students. Undergraduates develop a procedure for evaluating growth status, which involves the design of a simple demographic and family health questionnaire. The Penn students also train Turner students to take anthropometric data, such as lean body mass and fatness, which is then analyzed by the undergraduates. Undergraduates also teach nutrition to the Turner students.

Robert Giegengack teachers Environmental Studies 404-301, "Urban Environment: West Philadelphia." Undergraduate students in the course work with Turner students and faculty on projects to improve the environment in the surrounding neighborhoods, including those around Shaw Middle School. Education and outreach focus on lead toxicity and avoidance and also on appropriate household chemical disposal. I counted over twenty-four courses of this nature involving Penn students doing this kind of work in thirteen schools. In addition, Penn students assist in the community programs. At Shaw Penn students tutor middle school students. Middle school students also do service projects at elementary schools. According to Mr. D'Alfonso, the Penn community service program inspired the development of this program.

Third, these middle schools offer many interesting programs and feature block programs. At Turner, the students are organized into learning communities focusing on language arts and math and science. The block arrangement gives faculty freedom to arrange opportunities for the Penn students to teach special topics related to the curriculum areas, such as nutrition and environmental issues. Also the block model enables the middle school students to leave the building and participate in service activities at elementary schools. Shaw Middle School organize their communities into themes, two of which are computers and technology and environment and science. Ms. Davis's computer class, assisted by Penn students, produce a literary magazine. I visited with Pat Whack, a science teacher, who has worked with Penn students and her own students on environmental projects. They have planted a garden at the school, and the students are going to sell flowers and herbs. In a previous project, they sold bottled water to the students and staff at the school because the drinking water is not suitable for drinking.

Contrary to my assumption, I discovered that the WEPIC program is mainly responsible for keeping the keeping the community school concept alive. Ironically, the school district only gives nominal support to this concept. The district focus, much as it is across the country is only academic achievement. As I rode through the West Philadelphia, observing decrepit row houses, many of which are boarded up, rusted out cars, a man warming himself by a fire outside his house, few businesses, it is blatantly and tragically obvious that the social conditions of West Philadelphia, and other similar blighted communities in our major American cities that are the cause of school failure. Regardless of whether or not Harkavy realizes his desire of seeing the higher education/community school model as a means for transforming higher education, the Penn program is absolutely essential for enabling these public schools to provide a decent education for students. Joan Weeks mentioned that these schools lack sufficient books and school supplies, and that the teachers and the Penn students must create curriculum. Penn is providing a critical service to West Philadelphia and indeed is a model that should be replicated throughout all inner cities in the United States.

Minnesota—the University of Minnesota and Center for Citizenship Jane Addams School for Democracy and Central Lakes Community College Community Asset Building Model

The Jane Addams School for Democracy

Beginning in the fall 1996, University of Minnesota philosophy professor John Wallace, supported by Harry Boyte, director of the Humphrey Center for Democracy, founded the Jane Addams School for Democracy. Based on principles of public education elaborated and practiced by social worker Jane Addams in Chicago at the turn of the century, this "school" is an effort to launch community development efforts with Hmong and Hispanic groups at the Neighborhood House in the west side of St. Paul. The planning for this school occurred in the summer of 1996 by residents of the west side neighborhood and by individuals from the College of St. Catherine, a women's college in St. Paul, the University of Minnesota, and Neighborhood House, a settlement house in the neighborhood. Neighborhood House is a long established community center in the East Side neighborhood, and is currently funded through United Way. For over a hundred years, the West Side neighborhood immigrants have come to St. Paul to start their lives in the United States (Wallace, 1997, p. 17). A large number of recent immigrants from Southeast Asia and Latin America reside in this neighborhood. Neighborhood Houses has existed for one hundred years. Prior to the development of the Jane Addams School, the Neighborhood House has housed a variety of activities from child care to parenting classes and served as a meeting place for members of the community.

The individuals in the planning group for the Jane Addams School expanded the resources which they were able to bring to the neighborhood, going beyond the provision of services and moving in the direction of human development, community development, and empowerment. Wallace notes that settlement houses began with a strong emphasis on this kind of mission, but the realities of public policy have shifted community centers toward service delivery, resulting in a therapeutic, needs-based model, fostering client dependency rather than advocacy. The individuals in the planning group wanted to work at Neighborhood House in a way that would help restore a more asset-based approach and attempt simultaneously to reform undergraduate education "in the direction of making meaningful work with diverse others a key part of education" (Wallace, 1997, p. 7).

The planning group asked neighborhood residents what would they like to learn and if they would be interested in learning alongside college students. The residents identified several topics in which they were interested: English as a Second Language classes for the Hmongs, Hispanic members of the community "at the level of becoming able to think in the language and to discuss and work in a multi-lingual group that is addressing a substantive issue, and interest also in learning to write the new language" (p.18). Immigration and welfare reform was another topic of strong interest. They also expressed an interest in combining the learning of English with learning about U. S. history and government in order to prepare for the citizenship examination. These community members looked forward to working with college students. "Residents felt that they had a lot to learn from college students and professors—about substantive topics and about American culture—and that college students and professors also could learn a good deal from them, about their cultures and about their experiences of American life" (p.18).

Under the direction of Wallace, the Jane Addams School has deployed the "learning circle" model of the Highlander Folk School with three circles, a Hmong-English Circle, a Spanish-English circle, and a multi-cultural children's circle. University students can enroll in a one credit course, Directed Study in Philosophy or Philosophy 3970, receiving credit in exchange for participating in the learning circles and keeping a journal. On the night that I visited the Neighborhood House, a high school teacher and high school students also participated in the learning circles.

The concept of the learning circles is complex and subtle. People visit together sitting in a circle with a facilitated leader. The leader asks leading questions about topics that helps the group focus on pertinent issues and concerns. The leader begins the discussion by inviting everyone to respond to an opening question. Everyone is encouraged to participate. The circle discussion concept empowers everyone to participate in the learning process. This approach also builds a community of learners based on principles of equality and respect for the dignity of individuals.

These learning circles initially address the immediate needs of the Hmong and Hispanic members of the group. These two groups meet in separate but concurrent learning circles twice a week in the evenings for two hours. The participants work on English as a Second Language and study to pass the U.S. citizenship test. The class begins with members of the learning circle sharing personal and community concerns, after which they start work on their study tasks. English as a Second Language and citizenship preparation are just the starting point of the learning circle. Wallace envisions that as the group becomes more closely knit as a community, working in greater partnership with him and the students, members will begin to discuss other community concerns, such as the need for better paying jobs. This activity could lead to the development of a home-based business training program.

I observed the classes in progress as well as the multicultural children's circle. The latter also serves as an evening child-care program for the parents as they meet and study. The children also experience the learning circle concept, as they have a time for sharing and engage in a variety of learning and recreational activities. Again, service learning students work with the children in this learning circle.

In my visit at Jane Addams School, I saw all of the raggedness, noise, and uneven nature of the work that one would expect in this kind of activity. John Wallace is a strong leader and exhibits a caring attitude in the learning circles. The students worked diligently with the Hmong and Hispanic individuals as they studied English as a Second Language and engaged in citizenship preparation. A strong rapport existed between a number of the college students and the Hmongs and Hispanics.

Public Achievement

The Center for Democracy and Citizenship at University of Minnesota Humphrey Institute of Public Affairs, The Public Achievement Program and the city of St. Paul created the Public Achievement Program in 1990.[3] This program addressed a documented need of enabling young people to become involved in politics and public life. This program's goal is to educate young citizens to understand that they have the power to be creators of society, not simply consumers. The project strives to inspire citizens to be effective civic and political actors, and to take responsibility for the society in which they live.

Public Achievement involves young people in public work, the ongoing effort of working with a diverse group of people to make a lasting contribution and to solve public problems. Students choose a public issue that is important to them, then design projects that address the issue. Adult coaches guide the student groups in achieving their goals. Projects include creating a community park, changing school rules and regulations, organizing a high school child care center, and addressing community violence.

During 1997/1998 approximately two thousand elementary and high school students participated in Public Achievement, and roughly two hundred college students acted as coaches. In Minnesota, fifteen public and private schools participated in this program. Several colleges and universities supplied coaches, including Macalester College, Mankato State University, Metro State University, and the University of Minnesota. Also, an AmeriCorps group participated in this project.

Through this program young people have gained poise, ability to express themselves and listen to others, self-confidence, respect for peers of different ages, ability to use their own power effectively, problem solving skills, and perseverance. The college and university students have integrated their academic work with real world experience as they engaged in service learning. Boyte reports that all of his students from his last semester's public philosophy course have continued to serve as coaches after completion of their course. The school administration and teachers are enthusiastic about this program. One principal said, "Many kids are much better at expressing their interests and negotiating with teachers. Teachers have begun to base their teaching more directly on kids' interests" (Summary, 1998). Parents see an improvement in communication skills with their children and an enlargement of their child's interest in the community and the world.

Central Lakes College Community Asset Building Model

Karl Samp, coordinator of the service-learning program at Central Lakes College in Brainerd, Minnesota, received a grant in 1995 to address rural poverty. He looked at what his program could do in employing Kretzmann and McKnight's (1993) concept of community asset-building. This model historically had been used in urban areas, and Samp was interested in determining whether this model would work in an rural area.

Although I have previously highlighted the asset-based community development model created by Kretzmann and McKnight, further explanation is in order. This form of community development that departs from the Alinsky (1971) more confrontational model and particularly challenges what Kretzmann and McKnight describe as the deficit model, which is typified by the social service delivery system in place in local communities across the country. The deficit model generally views individuals and communities in terms of their problems and needs and often fosters an attitude of social service dependency. The community-asset model attempts to provide a corrective to the deficit approach by developing strategies of community development that build on individual and community assets as a mechanism for community development and improvement. Kretzmann and McKnight recommend a strategy of "asset inventories" to determine individual and community assets, such as vocational skills, useful for the internal development of low-income communities.

Samp and his team looked at Southeast Brainerd, the oldest community, and also the community having the highest rental rates, with only 30% owner-occupied homes in the neighborhood and a great many low-income individuals. Samp contacted people in the neighborhood who he thought might be key leaders to see if they had an interest in engaging in projects to improve their community. Historically, this neighbored built around a railroad yard. The area originally was called Frogtown because a large number of French-Canadian people had settled there. Once a fur trading and logging center, the paper mill at present is the largest employer in town, and the tourist industry also is economically important.

Samp contacted the president of a local bank and discovered that the bank had an interest in Southeast Brainerd. The bank had attempted to inform the community that rehab loans were available to spruce up the neighborhood, but the neighborhood should little interest. For a time the neighborhood had come together concerning an issue of a sexual predator. When this individual moved out, the fledgling community effort of solidarity subsided. Samp learned about this issue in discussions with the mayor and the councilperson from that neighborhood. The councilperson provided Samp with a list of about twenty-five names of people who might have an interest in the southeast neighborhood.

Samp invited people from the neighborhood to a meeting to discuss community issues. Twelve people attended. Samp and his team showed a brief video about the community-asset model. Samp and his associates also explained the asset-based community development model and discussed what was possible. The community members shared their concerns and thoughts about the neighborhood. They were concerned with the regressive nature of the neighborhood and also with public safety. Few people were acquainted with their neighbors. One woman who had attended a Quaker college and had strong belief in community suggested that people could barter their skills in the community. This might improve the community economically and socially. The group agreed that they wanted to continue meeting, and they wanted the college to play a leading role at that time.

First, the community held a holiday party so that people could get to know their neighbors. One federal work-study student from the college was assigned as a staff member to the neighborhood, and she helped organize the party. The Brainerd Redevelopment Authority also assisted in publicizing the party. The party was held in a local church. Forty-two people attended the party, including the mayor and community college members. The next activity was to plan a crime prevention workshop. Law and criminal justice students distributed information before holding this workshop. Police participated in the workshop and provided information about safe house programs, neighborhood watches, and general crime prevention. Fifty-five people attended, a combination of criminal justice faculty, students, neighborhood residents, and city council people.

Up to this point, Samp was the leader of this group. Mark Langseth, the Minnesota Campus Compact director, conducted an institute on the community-asset model, which was attended by several people from the college and the community. During this meeting Langseth explained that the college should not be "doing to or for" the community but instead should be working in a true partnership empowering neighborhood or other groups with which the college works. Samp felt that he had provided a strong leadership role, but decided he and his team needed to step back and encourage a neighborhood person to assume leadership of the group

The next activity several months later involved planning a major neighborhood clean-up day in the spring of 1996. Milo Mietzner, a work-study student in the environmental area, has also been working on developing a playground area. As result of the overall college and community partnership, Southeast Brainerd experienced a 40% decrease in the crime rate, reported a greater sense of community, and saw the community college as a valuable asset in helping improve community life. The neighborhood group formed as a nonprofit, the Southeast Brainerd Residents Association. This has led to a city-wide plan to develop six officially recognized neighborhood associations. Karl Samp and Vicki Blakesley, a sociology professor, created a course, Community Awareness and Activism, and people from the southeast neighborhood came into the class and discussed issues. Students have done asset-service projects geared toward helping the neighborhood develop a skill bank.

The Community College of Aurora

The Community College of Aurora's (CCA) Community and Work-force Development Program (CWDP) has laid the foundation for extending education as a comprehensive resource for the community in terms of workforce and economic development, wrap-around human resources, and community and civic leadership development. CCA's Community and CWDP, supported by President Larry Carter and Richard Tubbs, Dean of the CCA Lowry Campus, has drawn the college increasingly into community involvement.

Under my leadership as director of the CWDP, CCA is expanding its community outreach activities so that education will be a resource for all segments of the community. The CWDP is located at the Higher Education and Advanced Technology (HEAT) Education Campus at Lowry, formerly Lowry Air Force Base. The HEAT Center is developing a multicollege campus. CCA has established a branch campus at the HEAT campus, serving as the lead community college and providing general education courses for undergraduates and also some technology programs, including metrology (precision measurement) and biotechnology.

The CWDP involves a four-legged approach, with a comprehensive service-learning program, a family center providing social support services, a Center for Workforce Development, providing a variety of job training programs for economically disadvantaged individuals, including a worker-cooperative development program, and a community self-leadership initiative helping to empower community members and community-based organizations to engage in community improvement activities. The service-learning program contributes to a community development model of service learning by providing opportunities for students to contribute to the development of the CWDP's initiatives. This service-learning initiative served as the stimulus for creating our other community outreach programs described below

The Lowry Family Center, Kathy Hill-Young, Director

As of March 1, 1995, the family center provides a variety of resources for families in the Lowry community, including eighty-four formerly homeless families living at Lowry, the residents moving to Lowry, the residents surrounding Lowry, and CCA students. The family center offers a variety of workshops to help strengthen families and provides a referral service for families in need, from victim abuse to drug and alcohol treatment. The family center also offers a tutoring program for students and a parent support group.

Center for New Work, Daniela Mittoo, Coordinator

This program provides fast-track training—open-entry and open-exit accelerated skill training for dislocated workers, displaced homemakers, low income persons, and welfare recipients. The Center for New Work is developing a comprehensive job training program that can provide the training that for people based on an assessment of their level of job readiness. The Center for New Work provides one-on-one job counseling and placement. This program offers an essential skills in the workplace certificate, an administrative assistant program, a customer service program, and computer training. The Center for New Work has had a high success rate of placing individuals in jobs paying $8 to $11 an hour.

Center for Work Place Learning, Marguerite Stendquist and Becky Barcheski, Coordinators

This program was funded through a U. S. Department of Education grant to six community colleges through the Colorado Community College and Occupational Education System (CCCOES) to provide essential skills for the workplace for front-line employees in subjects such as English as a Second Language, Team Work, Problem Solving, and Computer Literacy. At the time of this writing, as far as I can determine, the CCA Center is the only one of these colleges offering for-credit training in essential skills. This program works in close partnership with the Center for New Work in which pre- and post-employment training for low-income individuals is provided for companies. These two programs are combining to develop a strong response to the new federal welfare reform program to help people on welfare obtain jobs that pay a living way. In addition, this Center is working in collaboration with some of the Aurora family centers to convert some of their trainings to college credit, which admittedly is good for the college. At the same time it is good for the individuals who participate in trainings at the family centers, because they can experience taking college courses, which can help boost self-esteem.

Community and Economic Development

Working in partnership with CCA's Center for Small Business Development, this initiative includes small businesses, home-based businesses, and worker cooperative training. The Early Childhood Education Division and the CWDP have developed a program to assist early childhood care providers in developing their own co-owned/employee-owned child care centers, where, for example, four or five child care providers could become co-owners of their own child care center. New Beginnings, the fourth such worker-owned day care center in the nation is about to open in Aurora. Childspace, a day care cooperative in Philadelphia has provided invaluable technical assistance to the New Beginnings group. This program will eventually expand to other occupations such as home health care providers, business building custodians, security guards, landscape and building maintenance workers, construction worker trades, and cosmetologists. In addition to worker cooperative training, low-income individuals can explore other options, such as creating a home-based business or a small sole proprietor business. Students in all of these programs study basic principles of business operation, including developing marketing business plans.

A Comprehensive Service Learning Program, Sharon Halford, Coordinator

Approximately twenty CCA faculty members currently offer service learning in their courses involving 250 students per semester. The Service Learning Program operates a placement service to assist students and faculty in service placement. Students are encouraged to engage in service activities in support of the Lowry Family Center. In one of the college's new initiatives. "Two Plus Four Equals Service on Common Ground," with the Campus Compact National Center for Community Colleges, which I have already mentioned previously, the service-learning program has formed a partnership with the University of Colorado-Denver (UCD). Beginning fall semester 1998 CCA and UCD students will be doing community service projects at the New Westside Economic Development Corporation (NEWSED), a non-profit community development corporation. The UCD students will be enrolled in Urban Citizen, taught by political science professors Jerry Jacks and Tony Robinson. CCA students will be enrolled in a similar community college course. The courses will be taught as one course on site at NEWSED. NEWSED staff also will be involved in the course, and students will engage in community development activities, including neighborhood beautification and other activities designed to get community members more politically involved.

I believe that an excellent direction for a community-development approach to service learning is developing college and university partnerships with nonprofit community economic development corporations, typified by NEWSED. Historically, most nonprofit community development corporations (CDC) have been involved in housing development more than economic development. But NEWSED breaks the mold, and in fact, is the main CDC in the Denver metro area that is involved in community economic development.

NEWSED was incorporated in 1973 as a not-for-profit community driven economic development corporation. Its primary focus has been to solve long-term economic problems in disadvantaged communities. This organization has created jobs for neighborhood residents, participated in neighborhood revitalization projects, provided employment and training services that promote self-sufficiency, developed shopping areas and services, fostered minority and neighborhood business ownership, increased home ownership and affordable rental opportunities, and hosted special cultural events and activities that showcase the neighborhood's predominantly Latino culture.[4]

In 1978, the City of Denver provided NEWSED with a $13.5 million Urban Development Action Grant that produced a $110 million residential and commercial development on a fourteen-acre tract of land near downtown Denver. The project comprises 958 units of middle-income housing, 100 units of elderly housing, a supermarket and an eleven-story office complex.

Since that time, NEWSED has built another shopping center, an automobile service center, and a retail complex. Its most recent real estate project includes the purchase and renovation of the Amic Moving and Storage Building that houses the organization and its self/record storage economic development venture. The two shopping centers were the first new retail and commercial developments in the neighborhood in twenty years.

NEWSED created the Santa Fe Drive Neighborhood Business Revitalization Area Program and the Santa Fe Drive Redevelopment Corporation (SFDRC) as mechanisms to promote economic development activity along the neighborhood's commercial corridor, Santa Fe Drive. SFDRC has developed and owns fourteen thousand square feet of parking for area businesses, a two thousand square foot service building to house a local bank and has completed eight city blocks of commercial streetscape improvements.

In 1995 NEWSED expanded its commercial revitalization activities to address the neighborhood's housing concerns. The neighborhood has experienced a decline in home ownership to the current rate of less than 15%, and there has been no recent housing production. Consequently, NEWSED is currently constructing the Palacio Inca apartment complex that will provide twelve new low-income apartment rental units. In addition, working with neighborhood residents, board and bank employee volunteers and donated labor and materials, NEWSED has completed basic and major repairs and improvements on fifteen homes owned by elderly residents. NEWSED is expanding these efforts and creating a home repair program that focuses on single family rehab projects. Also through the Barrio Aztlan Home Ownership Program, a collaboration among local lending institutions and other nonprofit organizations, NEWSED offers down payment and mortgage subsidy grant assistance for first-time homeowners. This initiative also provides homebuyer education workshops, pre-qualifying financial analysis, credit counseling, loan origination, post purchase counseling, and referrals to other lending institutions when appropriate. Over 150 families have used these services since the project's inception in September, 1995. The opportunity for UCD and CCA students to participate in service projects with NEWSED will undeniably provide unique opportunities for these two educational institutions to deepen and strengthen their community and civic development approaches to service learning.

Program for Citizenship and Leadership Training

This project received funding from CCCOES Kellogg Community Self-Leadership Project, directed by Michael Briand. A strong partner in this initiative has been the Aurora Project, a "healthy communities" type organization that works on developing strategic plans to help improve communities in the city of Aurora. The college has developed plans with several community-based organizations, including the Lowry, Crawford, Montbello, and South Family Centers. The college intends to use service-learning faculty and students in developing asset-based community development projects. One of the unique aspects of the CWDP plan involving service learning, is to focuses on community economic development, as previously indicated. Family centers will offer job training for college credit. Plans also exit through the family centers and other community-based organizations, such as the Latino Council and the neighborhood organization in "original Aurora" to develop worker cooperatives, home-based businesses; and eventually to address affordable housing initiatives, possibly through developing a non-profit community development corporation under the auspices of the college. Service-learning faculty and students will be encouraged to work on all aspects of these projects.

Finally, the fact that the CWDP is located at the Higher Education and Advanced Technology (HEAT) Center at Lowry, a former Air Force base, provides a growing range of jobs in advanced technology for those who are able to participate in this kind of training. Additional programs include the Rocky Mountain Manufacturing Academy (RMMA), which operates a cluster of programs, such as an advance machining program through Front Range Community College and other planned technology programs—semiconductor manufacturing, robotics, and photonics. Transitions, a new program, will enable women to obtain the necessary mathematical and scientific skills to secure a job in the technology field or enroll in one of these technology programs.

CONCLUSION

I wish to make several summative observations about the tentative Wingspread principles governing Campus and Community Partnerships. First, these principles emphasize the importance of creating "sustainable democratic urban communities." Moreover, it is important to promote "ongoing democratic process and approaches that emphasize increasing the capacity and power of the local community and its members." I consider this vision the "practical application" of the concept of promoting commonwealth practices in the community or a civic democracy approach. We must help grow local communities that are democratically empowered and sustainable. It should not be underestimated that we are interested in "sustainable" communities. I have claimed that I consider the civic literacy model of service-learning as one mode of community development aimed at promoting commonwealth. Community development does not always involve a higher education partnership, as exemplified by NEWSED's work. But community development work, whether or not it involves a higher education partner, must be democratically implemented, as true to the commonwealth tradition or citizen democracy. And equally true to this tradition, community development service learning must also mirror democratic practices.

As I discuss in the concluding chapter and have stated elsewhere, this form of community development work means more than communities practicing participatory democracy. This also means a community having the wherewithal to sustain itself. The unstated notion here is community economic development. Local community economic development is essential for a local urban community to be sustainable. As I have previously stated, community economic development has been neglected in the campus-community partnership effort. But this is reflective of the fact that to the extent that institutions of higher education are part of the equation, they tend to focus on education as a solution to the problems communities face. Institutions tend to lead with their obvious strengths. Community and economic development has not been the strength of institutions of higher education, especially four-year institutions. This "gap" will be overcome to the extent that the higher education institution truly works in a collaborative relationship, providing resources for helping to grow sustainable democratic urban communities through supporting the democratic empowerment of local communities—that is, providing the resources that can be made available from an institution of higher education in the service of this kind of community development. Institutions of higher education must at all costs avoid defining the problems and community needs in ways that are conducive to academic aproaches, such as policy research. A particular community may not need policy research.

As service-learning is deployed in the service of community development, colleges and universities must recognize when community service is peripheral to a community development project. Sometimes, service learning is not even needed. For example, if a community-based organization or neighborhood grant wants job training or assistance in the development of a community-owned business or a worker cooperative, students may only be marginally needed. Again, service-learning interests and needs should not define the community response. Granted, most community needs will have an education component, it is imperative that colleges and universities in these partnerships recognize when the problem or need requires non-academic resources or assistance. Although NEWSED typifies an organization that has achieved tremendous results without a great deal of higher education collaboration, NEWSED leaders are enthusiastic about the service learning partnership, because they feel that their success has at times distanced themselves from working closely with neighborhood members. They believe that the service-learning initiative will help regain this balance.

Lest I create the impression that I am recommending the standardization of service-learning around a community economic model, I must add that it is important to recognize service projects and community development activities must be designed to fit specific local needs. The examples I have presented in this chapter, I believe, are doing just that. The University of Minnesota effort is serving a special need of a local community. Brainerd Community College responded to the needs of a local neighborhood. The

Community College of Aurora serves the family centers, and the CCA/UCD project is responding to the needs of NEWSED.

The Penn WEPIC program serves the needs of West Philadelpha. They are help make the public schools in their partnership schools institutions that can educate young people enmired in an overwhelmingly ecomonically depressed community. This community typifies the observations of Wilson (1996) in his work *When Work Disappears: The World of the New Urban Poor*. Wilson claims that the effect of post-industrialization and the new global economy has essentially eliminated work from these urban ghettos. Wilson writes primaily about Chicago, but his remarks apply equally to Bronx, Detroit, Philadelphia, Washington, D.C. , and other major cities with large concentrations of poverty. He states, "The problems reported by the residents of poor Chicago neighborhoods are not a consequence of poverty alone. Something far more devastating has happened that can only be attributed to the emergence of concentrated and persistent joblessness and its crippling effects on neighborhoods, families, and individuals" (pp. 16-17). Wilson adds that neighborhoods experiencing high levels of joblessness are more likely to experience low levels of social organization. "High rates of joblessness trigger other neighborhood problems that undermine social organization, ranging from crime, gang violence, and drug trafficking to family breakups and problems in the organization of family life" (p. 21). Wilson observes that "high rates of neighborhood poverty are less likely to trigger problems of social organization if the residents are working"(p. 23).

The circumstances of the underclass in communities such as West Philadelphia overwhelm me. Welfare reform aggravates the situation of these communities. At the time of the printing of this book, people who are on the Temporary Aid for Need Families program, which replaced the Aid for Families with Dependent Children, now have only four years remaining for public assistance. They have a five year lifetime limit. With virtually no jobs in these inner city neighborhoods, what will these people do when welfare runs out? What will happen to these cities?

Programs like Penn's are providing an absolutely neceessary service to sustaining decent public education in these communitiies. But what will hapen four years from now, if there are no jobs created in these urban communities, where there is hardly any work at the present time? As a suggestion, I think that it is important for more stable communities, who are not as burdened with such deep-seated poverty, to begin to create economic prototypes that can be developed in communities such as West Philadelphia. Places such as Denver, Seattle, and Minneapolis, which are not as beset with such severe poverty rates, are in a much better position to move forward with community economic development. I believe that these communities should concentrate on developing strong worker cooperative models and other forms of community economic development. They should target the service economy, such as day care, home care, building and home maintence, temporary hiring agencies, security guards, and cosmetologists, striving to create worker-owned businesses that can provide living wages. Colleges and universities can play a major role in developing models of community-economic development. Service-learning students can assist in all phases of the development of such initiatives. In turn, these models can be disseminated to cities where more concentrated pockets of poverty exist.

Finally, we must work on continuous change of higher education institutional structures to enable higher education to be more responsive to community needs. I believe that this need requires a shift in the paradigm of the way we see institutions of higher education responding to the community, from a higher education-driven paradigm to a community-driven paradigm. I conclude with this topic.

NOTES

1. The conference called these principles "Working Guidelines for Community-Higher Education Partnerships." I have used the language of the National Campus Compact that is working on a similar endeavor, "Campus and Community Partnerships." I wish to thank Ira Harkavy who generously shared with me his draft of these principles.

2. Wingspread, designed by Frank Lloyd Wright, is the former home of the H. F. Johnson family. Wingspread is now a conference center operated by the Johnson undation and hosts a variety of meetings annually. Community building currently is one of the areas of interest.

3. Thanks to Harry Boyte and Elaine Eschenbacher at Center for Democracy and Citizenship for information about the Public Achievement Program. Some of the information is a duplication of their program description.

4. Information supplied by UCD Professor Tony Robinson and NEWSED.

10

The Social Responsibilities of Higher Education

In this chapter I hope to pull together the threads of this book as they bear on the issue of the social responsibilities of higher education. I suggest, in line with previous chapters, that higher education has an ethical and social responsibility to utilize its resources to help strengthen the local democratic process in the service of improving community life. Of course, there are obvious criticisms to this approach, and I want to devote this chapter to dealing with those criticisms and position my arguments in terms of the latest thinking regarding campus and community collaboration.

It has taken our society a long time to get into its existing situation, and it will probably take a long time for significant changes to occur. Higher education historically has contributed to the development of our society's strengths and weaknesses. Education in general, and higher education in particular, historically has served the reigning political and economic powers. At the same time, in the last half of the twentieth century, a case can be made that the university has become something of a power unto itself and yet also faces a legitimacy crises.

A BRIEF HISTORY

In the 1700s colleges served the needs of the church to provide ministers and later teachers (Smith, 1990). Early in the history of the formation of the university, beginning with Thomas Jefferson, a debate waged about the role of education as contributing to progress and scientific development, with traditionalists wanting to preserve the past. Jefferson, who sided with the civic republican tradition, nevertheless supported the scientific and enlightenment approach to education. In the nineteenth century, the German ideal of a university "dedicated to research conducted by the specialized professor with the help of student apprentices" emerged (Bok, 1982). This model existed alongside the British model, which emphasized undergraduate education that included moral and emotional as well as intellectual development. Bok points out that the American university differed from its European counterparts in seeing education as serving the needs of workforce and business development.

Tycoons, such as Ezra Cornell, and Leland Stanford, who wanted to make their mark through developing educational edifices of power and prestige, influenced the path from a more traditionalist model to a more pragmatic model of higher education. During the period between the end of the Civil War and the first decade of the twentieth century, the university provided research oriented to serving the needs of business and agricultural development supported capital. An important exception to this approach was Johns Hopkins University under the leadership of President Daniel Coit Gilman, who was the guiding force behind the organization of the Charity Organization Society and who endeavored to integrate social welfare work into the curriculum (Harkavy, 1996, p. 8). In other universities, professors who spoke out in criticism of the shortcomings of capitalism were banished from the universities or generally suppressed, resulting in an inward turn on the part of the professorate working in the humanities and the social sciences.

The Morrill Act, passed in 1862, provided federal land for the creation of state universities and community colleges. Some state colleges already existed prior to the Morrill Act, and this legislation enabled these institutions, such as Wisconsin, Michigan, and Minnesota, to expand greatly. These state universities shared a vision with places like Johns Hopkins and Clark University of "mind as being in the service of society, although they were also more practically oriented in terms of careers" (Page, 1990, p. 62). During this period the battles of labor, as reflected in the populist movement and the efforts of the Knights of Labor, fanned the efforts of professorate critics, such as Edward Bemis, about the negative consequences of capitalism. But this was suppressed. Social criticism was regarded as unscientific. Smith (1990) explains, "'Scientific' meant 'objective, dispassionate, neutral'" (p. 76). He continues:

It soon became evident that owners of the new universities had no interest in seeing them used as engines of reform. The owners were content with things as they were.

Any substantial changes were apt to be to their disadvantage. They had not contributed their millions to raise up a nest of academic vipers ready to bite the hand that fed them. (p. 76)

Professors in the United States, unlike their European counterparts, increasingly were viewed, not as scholars, but as employees of business-dominated boards of trustees and regents. This business ethos fostered intense rivalries between universities and increasing bureaucratization.

The Progressive Era spawned some important efforts of the university to address community problems. Seth Low, president of Columbia from 1890 to 1901, had a compelling vision of university-city relationships (Harkavy, 1996, p. 9). Perhaps the most important example was the University of Chicago, which had close ties with Hull House, founded by Jane Addams and Ellen Starr on Chicago's West Side in 1889. Harkavy observes: "Adopting a multifaceted institutional approach to the social problem of the immigrant groups in the Nineteenth Ward, Hull House residents offered activities along four lines designated by Addams as the social, educational, humanitarian, and civic" (p. 9).

Labor Union activities took place at Hull House, which also served as a forum for social, political, and economic reform (Harkavy, p. 10). Sociologists from the University of Chicago were closely associated with Hull House. The University of Chicago's first president, William Rainey Harper, envisioned his institution as providing service for mankind, "whether within scholastic walls or without those walls and in the world at large" (Harkavy, p. 10). Despite the examples, of Chicago and a few other universities, Harkavy points out that, in most cases, "Progressive Era university presidents and academics had an expert-driven model of change founded on the assumption that the expert, with scientific knowledge in hand, would increase efficiency in governmental agencies and design institutions that improve the quality of life for the urban poor and immigrant" (1996, p. 8).

The outbreak of World War I severely challenged the faith in scientific progress. The entire edifice of education, research, and scholarship was called into question (Smith, 1990). However, many people considered academic critics of the war unpatriotic, and these critics were suppressed. The American Association of University Professors supported this kind of criticism.

President Woodrow Wilson enlisted the help of scholars in trying to achieve world peace and improve social conditions, and some academics begin to hope again. But these hopes were soon dashed in the failure of the Versailles Treaty. Smith (1990) speculates that the continued failure of the intellectual life to bring about great societal changes contributed to the disposition of professors to withdraw ever further into their "scientific" researches. "A natural consequence was that the researches became more and more for their own sake, for the sake of research itself, and less with the intention of improving the world" (p. 130).

The contemporary university was established in the twentieth century. These universities created departments that rivaled one another for faculty positions. Faculty positions were generally financed by the large lecture hall format. Professors lectured to large numbers of students, aided by graduate teaching assistants, who conducted discussion groups and graded exams. A typical professor would offer a couple of large lecture classes a year and then teach small upper-level and graduate courses and conduct research. Professors' salaries were essentially paid for by the large lecture classes, which, of course, constituted the majority of the courses taken by freshman and sophomores. And, of course, the trend continues today, except that an increasing number of adjunct or part-time professors are doing the brunt of the large lecture teaching.

Sullivan (1996) points out that in the later part of the twentieth century the role of the university centered on scientific research. Sullivan states, "Especially since World War II, the greatest expansion of the universities' influence on American life has reinforced the idea that expertise means the ability to apply scientific knowledge to the tasks and problems of life" (p. 19). The university, especially during the post–World War II era, served as an engine of technological advance that produced tremendous economic growth. At the same time, it also trained a "national meritocratic elite, significantly contributing to upward social mobility" (p. 20).

The development of higher education as we know it has never been without its critics. At various times, critics from within the university have spoken out against the tendency of higher education to serve corporate America, but these critics have been silenced as often as they have been raised. The period of the Vietnam War was a time when higher education came under its harshest criticism. College students themselves rose in protest, viewing the multiuniversity as being part of the military industrial complex. Some critics, such as Paul Goodman and Ivan Illich, called for a radical change in or even abandonment of the universities as we know them. Although these attacks waned with the end of the Vietnam War, the university as we know it remains a target of criticism.

VIEWS REGARDING THE SOCIAL RESPONSIBILITY OF HIGHER EDUCATION

With this historical backdrop in mind, I would like briefly to summarize some of the standard views regarding the social responsibility of the university and then look toward developing trends. Bok (1982) suggests that there are three positions one might take regarding the social responsibilities of the university. While I agree with his criticism of the first two positions, I think that his own recommendation, the third position, has serious shortcomings. I briefly review these criticisms and then develop an alternative position for the role of higher education from the commonwealth perspective.

The Traditionalist Critique

Traditionalists, such as Jacques Barzun, Robert Nisbet, and Sidney Hook, offer two lines of argument. One is the claim that "the wholesale efforts to serve society's needs has exposed higher education to pressures and temptation that threaten to corrupt academic values" (Bok, 1982, p. 67). As a result, campuses foster countless research projects that could be conducted by business and industry, and professors spend too much time serving as corporate consultants. Teaching loads continue to decrease, resulting in the use of more graduate students to teach undergraduates. The search for basic knowledge is weakened in favor of knowledge that is of immediate practical use.

A second traditionalist criticism is that service-oriented universities will be pressured continually to expand their range of services and activities, further diluting the core academic mission of teaching and research. Many small bureaucracies will proliferate within the university as various programs are created to serve external needs. This bureaucracy will be consumed with rescuing floundering programs. Students will fall through the cracks, receiving even less attention than they do under a less service-oriented system.

Bok (1982) replies that the critics are so concerned with purifying the traditional mission that the result would be an even more cloistered university, paying even less attention to social problems. Moreover, for universities to adhere to the traditionalist mission, they probably would have to eliminate professional schools, because those are very much practically oriented. However, this would diminish the academic rigor of professional schools, which benefit from their ties to the university. Bok questions the idea that "pure research" advances knowledge over research linked to finding solutions for the problems of our society. Bok and also Smith (1990) both contend that research, especially in the humanities, is often trivial and self-referential. "If professors lose some of their objectivity by trying to shape the society they purport to describe, they have also gained something in experience and first-hand knowledge" (Bok, 1982, p. 74). Bok concludes: "the cloistered university could probably exist only at a heavy cost to the quality of professional education applied research, social criticism, and expert advice—activities that are all important to our society" (p. 73).

The Activist Critique

The activists maintain that the professed liberal neutrality of the university is specious. Rather than upholding the principle of disinterested research, universities in fact at best tacitly endorse the status quo and support initiatives defined by the wealthy and the powerful (Bok, 1982, p. 79). This response to society deprives higher education of the claim to intellectual leadership, while it encourages involvement in activities of dubious ethical and intellectual value. For example, research sponsored by pharmaceutical companies with a vested interest in seeing their products determined to be safe is a case in point. Community colleges locate companies on their campuses, which they use as teaching sites. At worst, under the banner of liberal neutrality, higher education not merely reinforces the status quo but actively engages in reproducing the corporate capitalist structure.

While supporting the notion of a more socially responsible university, Bok is critical of the radicals recommendation of strong campus and community collaboration. In the first place, according to Bok, further professorial engagement in the community may mean that professors will have even less time to spend with students. Bok also questions whether professors have the expertise needed to attack the problems of society. He comments: "even the hardiest optimist has to wonder whether many professors possess the practical knowledge and political skill to make much lasting progress in attacking the problems of urban poverty, deteriorating schools, and hard-core unemployment" (1982, p. 82). Bok points out that academic research and political action are equally demanding activities. It is doubtful, Bok comments, that the professorate could carry out both tasks equally well. He believes that we probably could assist the economically disadvantaged in our society more by helping improve the social agencies that serve them rather than professors becoming involved in such efforts.

Bok's final concern returns to the issue of liberal neutrality. He asks whose social interest should be served by the university? We assume that it is the interests of the poor or those historically who have been victims of discrimination. By why these interests? Could not the professors become activist supports of right-wing groups or corporate America? On what grounds can one interest group be the object of research attention to the exclusion of other interest groups?

Bok attempts, I think unsuccessfully, to forge a middle path between the traditionalist and the activist extreme. He believes that the university should engage in policy research aimed at addressing the social problems of the day. But Bok contends that a distinction must be drawn between providing policy research aimed at addressing the problems of poverty and developing programs that attempt to reduce poverty. Universities also should avoid undertaking tasks that nonacademic organizations can perform better. Bok recognizes that some more practically oriented programs may be appropriate for higher education, but these should be performed by local community colleges or state colleges (1982, p. 77).

Another important principle, new ventures should enhance the institution's teaching and research activity. Bok cites as an example teaching hospitals. Teacher practicums would be another example. Finally, Bok contends that projects should not be approved without faculty endorsement. He states: "In my experience, many of the greatest programmatic failures in universities have occurred when a dean or president has identified an important opportunity and received substantial funding without first ascertaining whether able professors are actually willing to devote substantial time and effort to the enterprise" (p. 77).

PUBLIC SCHOLARSHIP

A number of influential thinkers have began to call for a different role of higher education (Boyer, 1994, 1996; Checkoway, 1997; Coye, 1997; Harkavy, 1991, 1996a; Matthews, 1996). It is a role in which, instead of relying on the model of applied scientific research, higher education should begin to address the needs of strengthening the civic infrastructure. Sullivan (1996) states that the kind of expertise now needed is civic rather than technical in orientation. He writes: "This sort of expert contributes to the civic purpose not by circumventing the public through the imposition of technical devices, but by engaging with broader publics, attempting to make sense of what is happening, analyzing the working of our complex systems with reference to values and principles, listening, arguing, persuading, and being persuaded" (p. 21). Instead of "applied research," the present calls for "something more like active partnership and shared responsibility in addressing problems whose moral and public dimension are openly acknowledged" (p. 21).

At the end of his life, Earnest Boyer (1996) also advocated the development of the "New American College" that would emphasize public scholarship, the notion that teaching and research would be directed toward addressing the great social problems that we face. Coye (1997), a former researcher for the Carnegie Foundation, attempts to summarize the emerging conception of the New American College envisioned by Boyer. Boyer and others, such as Frank Wong, have influenced the development of an organization, The Association of New American Colleges that now has a membership of 21 colleges under the leadership of William G. Berbeet. This organization meets semiannually "to share ideas and stimulate good practice around the goals that Boyer and Wong articulated" (Coye, 1997, p. 23). As reiterated by Coye, the conception of the New American College is founded on three priorities. First, we should clarify the curriculum. We should develop a general education core based on "those experiences, relationships, and ethical concerns that are common to all of us simply by virtue of our membership in the human family at a particular moment on history"(p. 24). Curricular revision should focus on more interdisciplinary efforts. Also courses would be delivered in nontraditional ways, "spilling out into the community" (p. 25). Service learning would be a central aspect of this kind of education.

A second notion is that of connecting to the world beyond the classroom. Teaching and scholarship should be devoted to addressing the social problems that surrounds us in our communities. Students and faculty should be involved in community service efforts aimed at improving community life. Faculty could teach their courses in the community as they and their students work on community projects. Traditional research would yield to community action research aimed at improving community life.

Finally, colleges should themselves become true communities. According to Coye, institutions of higher education should work more deliberately toward developing a campus atmosphere in which students and scholars are committed to common values, which would presumably be democratic in character and supportive of the values of public scholarship. Coye believes that, in the absence of working deliberately to create campus community, higher education is in danger of further fragmentation due to the increasing reliance on part-time faculty and to distance learning. College students can now obtain degrees through the Internet. Educators must answer the question, "Why should students continue to obtain their education on a college campus?" The answer must be, according to Coye, something like "'Because the life of the college provides something you can't get off campus.' Although you can learn a great deal about human values from the family, church, or even from a computer screen, college should be about *actively exploring* values and living them" (p. 26).

We are clearly at a historical point where service learning has not merely contributed to the moral development of young people, but it is helping reengage institutions of higher education with the larger society in ways that are relevant to the times and circumstances we are facing. I regard the efforts of the Association of the New American College as a positive sign. The National Campus Compact also is moving in this direction.

It would be nice to end on a cheery note in which we can predict that all of this effort will be able to transform higher education and, in turn, our communities. But this would be incredibly naive. While I am extremely hopeful, I am concerned about the direction that some of this public scholarship has taken. I see two areas of concern. One is the undertow of traditionalism within higher education, or what Smith (1990) calls "academic fundamentalism," and the other involves the often elitist assumptions surrounding the formation of campus and community partnerships.

First, traditionalism. In a recent essay, K. Mattson and M. Shea (1997) see signs that service learning is in danger of being appropriated as merely a tool of traditional academic applied research. I critiqued this tendency in my chapter on experiential education. The authors suggest that the "professionalization" of service learning constitutes evidence of this direction of service learning. In some colleges and universities, students can now major in this subject and even do graduate work in service learning. Mattson and cite the American Association of Higher Education monograph series linking service learning to academic disciplines as an example of the current tendency to legitimize service learning in traditional terms, as no more than experiential learning.

As the coeditor of the philosophy volume in this series, I must concede that I share some of these concerns. However, two sides to this issue exist. Service learning may be appropriated by traditionalism. However, the possibility exists that if service learning is seen as a way to enhance the traditional disciplines, more faculty will embrace it as a pedagogical tool. And I am absolutely confident, based on working in this movement at the national level for a number of years, that service learning can be the means of drawing faculty and students into their communities. Through service learning faculty come to realize that their teaching and research can take on a new life and that "real" problems in the community can be addressed in discipline appropriate ways.

Having said this, I have seen time and time again, and especially among faculty within four-year institutions of higher education, service learning used mainly to provide direct service, the volunteer mode, which I have already criticized. The tug of traditionalism is powerful, especially for entrenched university professors. Some in the public scholarship camp have maintained that the only way this will change is if the tenure and reward system is changed in such a way as to provide greater recognition of the value of community service for faculty, alongside the traditional values of teaching and research. Junior faculty, who attain tenureship through traditional research, are not going to devote much of their time to working with their students in the community. These faculty simply must publish articles and books if they are going to obtain tenure. Faculty are put into a perverse situation in which faculty and administration provide rhetorical support for service learning but give no real regard for service-learning activities when it comes time to determine whether a professor will be awarded tenure. So faculty role and reward changes are urgently needed.

I suspect that the deeper problem is the very notion of campus and community partnerships. Many advocates of public scholarship, such as Harkavy and Sullivan, maintain that we fundamentally need to change higher education itself to make it more relevant to our communities. I thoroughly support this call for institutional reform. But I am skeptical that higher education can achieve its own reform in a self-referential way. When one surveys the history of the development of higher education, as I have done briefly, it becomes all too clear that higher education has emerged in response to social needs and pressures. By the very nature of the beast, higher education has served the interests of business and the market economy. Unless fundamental social transformation occur, I doubt that higher education will change its modus operandi very much. It is likely that higher education will absorb service learning into academic traditionalism as Mattson and Shea warn. Despite the Association of the New American College, there is every evidence academic business will go on as usual.

We could well see the failure of many state colleges and small private colleges over the next decade as a college degree offered on a traditional campus becomes too expensive. Students may indeed turn to colleges that reduce their overhead and tuition costs through replacing faculty with computer-based instruction and distance learning. The growth of adjunct faculty, who have no due process rights or tenure, undermine the political capacity of faculty governing bodies to challenge these cost-saving measures. Nor can part-time faculty effectively challenge academic fundamentalism. Further, four-year institutions of higher education may be unable to turn out graduates with the kind of degrees appropriate to the needs of the job market, as students turn to community colleges and proprietary certificate programs.

Perhaps service learning can restore teaching relevance to the classroom, and serve as a counter-measure to these high-tech learning options. But there is something almost ludicrous about the prospect of elite universities transforming themselves into community-engaged institutions as they continue primarily to provide the means for students to take up elite positions in a society that reinforces a corporate capitalist culture, which has undermined our communities. So where do we turn?

I wish to conclude by making several recommendations about how I believe that service learning and campus and community partnerships can be forces not only for social change but for change within higher education. I believe that the most fundamental paradigm shift we need is to understand the community—not the university—as the engine of reform. This paradigm shift goes against our liberal historical tendency to regard education as the means of social improvement. But clearly many of us doubt that education has played this role during the turmoil of the 1960s. And what does it mean for higher education to view the community as the engine of reform?

In the first place, it means that we need to take the commonwealth, strong democracy, or civic republican tradition very seriously. We need to look to enlisting the resources of higher education, alongside other significant community partners, to strengthen the local civic infrastructure. A number of writers such as Boyte have important ideas about what must be done. For Boyte this means engaging in public work. An example of public work is simply to do community projects that help improve community life. It means to help reforge a sense of what it means to be a "public citizen."

But I do not think that working toward developing a sense of the public takes us far enough. Beyond this, we must work with local community-based organizations in helping them develop projects to improve community life. We have pressing needs of affordable housing, child care, and community economic development that need to be addressed in every community. Welfare reform is bringing many of these needs to a crisis point. We live in a time of unprecedented employment and economic growth, yet we face unprecedented gaps between the haves and have-nots. Low-paying jobs are abundant. As we shift welfare recipients into the workforce, many are condemned to a life of dispiriting struggle, constantly facing the needs of child care and finding affordable housing and worrying about a time when there will be no welfare benefits to provide them with a safety net. And what will those who are the lowest paid do if we have an economic downturn and massive layoffs? If these layoffs do not come because of an economic downturn, greater computerization will see to it that more workers than ever are replaced by automation.

At the same time, we witness an increasingly disconnected and angry shrinking middle-class people who are finding themselves downsized, often moved into temporary employment without retirement and medical benefits. Our civic disconnection is linked, not only to our discouragement about big government, but to our suspicion that things are out of control and that there is little we can do to reverse the situation. Unless we begin to find ways to address the growing gap between the wealthy and the poor in our society, we will find an increasing right-wing turn among our shrinking middle-class as they feel themselves threatened by an increasingly desperate underclass and a remote corporate elite.

In the face of the emerging crisis, calling for a rebuilding of our local civic infrastructure through increasing our capacity of public deliberation, as many civic republicans advocate, is insufficient. Increasing our capacity for local democratic decision making, is necessary. But participatory democracy at the local level will not increase unless the democratic process addresses our pressing concerns of affordable housing, child care, and community economic development. We must promote civically-based community economic development.

This need presents a great opportunity for higher education, for clearly our colleges and universities possess the resources for helping communities tackle these problems. But this must be done through a spirit of campus and community collaboration. Our colleges and universities must abandon the mode of coming to the table with a technological focus. Such a focus arrogantly suggests that because the university has some of the resources with which to address community problems, these resources should be the ones to solve the problems. But the main problem is not technological in nature: It is one of vision about the good life for a community. We must discover how to enlist the necessary civic participation to attack the problems. And it also is about using this civic engine to work on the urgent problems.

If all of these problems are addressed in a democratic and participatory way, I believe that real progress can result. I think we need not worry about Bok's suggestion that if higher education begins to work in the community to attack practical problems, the university may be at the mercy of undemocratic requests. It is important that the campus-community collaborations be modeled on a process of participatory democracy. This will ensure that demagogues can not manipulate the community or its higher education partners.

I wish to conclude by saying something about the important role that community colleges can play in this civic endeavor. Smith (1996), who otherwise offers up a devastating critique of higher education, states: "there are community colleges, where thousands of able and intelligent men and women take their teaching opportunities with the greatest seriousness and give more than value received. These institutions, with close ties to their parent communities, free for the most part of the snobbish pursuit of the last academic fads that so warp their university counterparts, and free also of the unremitting pressure to publish or perish, are, I believe, the hope of higher education in America." (pp. 19–20).

As a practitioner of service learning and an advocate of community, workforce and economic development in a community college, I share this optimism. Historically, as Vaughan (1982) has described, the community and junior colleges emerged with a mission to provide affordable higher education for students within local communities and to support the job training and other educationally relevant needs of the community. The community outreach mission has been significantly reinforced by a report of the Commission on the Future of Community Colleges, *Building Communities: A Vision for a New Century* (1988). This document defines "community" as not only a region to be served, "but also as a climate to be created" (p. 7). The documents states:

Building communities is, we believe, an especially appropriate objective for the community college because it embraces the institution's comprehensive mission. But the goal is not just *outreach*. Perhaps more than any other institution, the community college also can inspire *partnerships* based upon shared values and common goals. The building of community, in its broadest and best sense, encompasses a concern for the whole, for integration and collaboration, for openness and integrity for inclusiveness and self-renewal. (p. 7)

As Parsons and Lisman (1996) indicate, this document has led to a strong effort among community colleges to work more actively through service learning and other means to help revitalize the civic life of local communities and improve community life.

Much remains to be done. But I am firmly convinced that if we shift our attention from educational reform to community reform through the participatory democratic process, we shall see educational reform as a consequence of community reform. Some academic critics of this approach may be leery of the ability of the community to affect such a change. But we must remember that we are the community, academics, professionals, business leaders, family members, church members, and others. We must find our resources for community revitalization from wherever we can. Some of those resources, indeed many of them, will be located within our institutions of education.

I have a strong faith in the capacity of goodness, and I believe that our intellectual capital can be utilized in the service of strengthening social and civic capital. There are plenty "models" of how we might address our urgent problems. We can grow local economies through developing worker cooperatives and employee-owned businesses, we can even develop community-owned business. We can help provide affordable housing through the development of limited equity co-owned housing in which people can own condos, apartments, and homes with minimal investments. We can address issues of child care through the development of employee-owned day care centers, which, as I have stated, already is happening in several places across the country. And many other community-based solutions can be found for the problems that besiege us. It merely takes a willingness for all of us to come together as concerned members of the community, with a willingness to work through the democratic process to find collective solutions to our problems. And in this process we can transform communities and higher education.

Works Cited

Adams, L. B. (1993). How one school builds self-esteem and serves the community. *Middle School Journal* 24 (5), 53–55.

Adams, F. T., and Hansen, G. B. (1993). *Putting democracy to work: A practical guide for starting and managing worker-owned businesses.* Rev. ed. San Francisco: Berrett-Koehler Publishers.

Alinsky, S. D. (1971). *Rules for radicals: A pragmatic primer for realistic radicals:* New York: Vintage Books.

Anyon, J. (1988). Schools as agencies of social legitimation. In W. F. Pinar, ed., *Contemporary curriculum discourses* (pp. 175–200). Scottsdale, AZ: Gorsuch Scarisbrick.

Apple, M. W. (1979). *Ideology and curriculum.* London: Routledge & Kegan Paul.

Apple, M. W. (1982/1985). *Education and power.* Boston: Ark Paperbacks.

Apple, M. W. (1989). *Teachers and texts: A political economy of class and gender relations in education.* New York: Routledge.

Astin, A. W. The role of service in higher education. *About Campus* 1 (1),14–21.

Ballantine, J. H. (1989/1983). *The sociology of education: A systematic analysis.* Englewood Cliffs, NJ: Prentice Hall.

Barber, B. R. (1984). *Strong democracy.* Berkeley: University of California Press.

Barber, B. R. (1992). *An aristocracy of everyone: The politics of education and the future of America.* New York: Ballantine Books.

Barr, R. B., and Tagg, J. (1995, November/December). From teaching to learning: A new paradigm for undergraduate education. *Change* 27 (6), 13–25.

Batchelder, T. H., and Root, S. (1994). Effects of an undergraduate program to integrate academic learning and service: Cognitive, prosocial cognitive, and identity outcomes. *Journal of Adolescence* 17, 341–355.

Bellah, R. N., Madsen, R., Sullivan, W. M., Swidler, A., and Tipton, S. M. (1985). *Habits of the heart: Individualism and commitment in American life.* New York: Harper and Row, Publishers.

Bellah, R. N., Madsen, R., Sullivan, W. M., Swidler, A., and Tipton, S. M. (1991). *The good society.* New York: Alfred A. Knopf.

Benn, S. I., and Peters, R. S. (1959). *Social principles and the democratic state.* London: George Allen and Unwin.

Bennett, K. P. and LeCompte, M. D. (1990). *The way schools work: A sociological analysis of education.* White Plains, NY: Longman.

Benson, L., and Harkavy, I. (1991). Progressing beyond the welfare state. In L. Benson and I. Harkavy, eds. *Universities and community schools* (pp. 3–28). Philadelphia: University of Pennsylvania Press.

Bok, D. (1982). *Beyond the ivory tower: Social responsibilities of the modern university.* Cambridge, MA: Harvard University Press.

Bok, D. (1990). *Universities and the future of America.* Durham, NC: Duke University Press.

Boss, J. (1994). The effect of community service work on the moral development of college ethics students. *Journal of Moral Education* 23 (2), 183–198.

Bowles, S., and Gintis, H. (1976). *Schooling in capitalist America: Educational reform and the contradictions of economic life.* New York: Basic Books, Inc.

Boyd, D. (1980). The condition of sophomoritis and its educational cure. *Journal of Moral Education* 10 (1), 24–39.

Boyer, E. L. (1994, March 9). Creating the new American college. *The Chronicle of Higher Education,* 40 (27), A48.

Boyer, E. L. (1996). The scholarship of engagement. *Journal of Public Service and Outreach* I (1), 11–20.

Boyte, H. C. (1991, June). Community Service and Civic Education. *Phi Delta Kappan* 72, 765–767.

Boyte, H. C. (1989). *CommonWealth: A return to citizen politics.* New York: The Free Press.

Boyte, H. C., and Farr, J. (1997). The work of citizenship and the problem of service-learning. In R. Battistoni and W. Hudson, eds., *Experiencing citizenship: Concepts and models for service-learning in political science* (pp. 25–48). Washington, DC: American Association for Higher Education.

Boyte, H. C. , and Kari, N. N. (1996). *Building America: The democratic promise of public work.* Philadelphia: Temple University Press.

Briand, M. (In press). *Practical politics: Five principles for a politics that works.* Urbana and Chicago: University of Illinois Press.

Bricker, D. C. (1989). *Classroom life as civic education: Individual achievement and student cooperation in schools.* New York: Teachers College Press.

Building communities: A vision for a new century. (1988). A report of the Commission on the Future of Community Colleges. Washington, DC: American Association of Community Colleges.

Bullard, R. C. (1997). *Dismantling racism in the policy arena: The role of collaborative social research.* In P. Nyden, A. Figert, M. Shibley, and D. Burrows, eds., *Building community: Social science in action* (pp. 67–73). Thousands Oaks, CA: Pine Forge Press.

By the people: An AmeriCorps citizenship and service training guide. (1995). Minnesota Commission on National and Community Service and the Center for Democracy and Citizenship, Humphrey Institute of Public Affairs, Minneapolis, MN.

Checkoway, B. (1997, February). Reinventing the research university for public service. *Journal of Planning Literature* 2 (3), 307–319.

CIRP Press Release. 1997. Http://www.gseis.ucla.edu/heri/press97.htm.

Civic declaration: A call for a new citizenship. (December, 1994). An Occasional Paper of the Kettering Foundation

Cohen, J., and Kinsey, D. (1994). "Doing good" and scholarship: A service-learning study. *Journalism Education* 48 (4), 4–14.

Coles, R. (1993). *The call of service: A witness to idealism.* Boston: Houghton Mifflin.

Coye, D. (1997, May/June). Ernest Boyer and the new American college: Connecting the "disconnects." *Change* 29 (3), 21–29.

Crowner, D. (1992). The effects of service-learning on student participants. Paper presented at the National Society for Experiential Education Conference, Newport, RI.

Daly, M., ed. (1994). *Communitarianism: A new public ethics.* Belmont, CA: Wadsworth Publishers.

Dewey, J. (1956). *The child and the curriculum and the school and society.* Rev. ed. Chicago: The University of Chicago Press, 1956.

Dewey, J. (1922/1957). *Human nature and conduct.* New York: The Modern Library.

Dewey, J. (1927/1991). *The public and its problems.* Athens, OH: Swallow Press.

Dewey, J. (1938). *Experience and education.* New York: Macmillian Publishing Co., Inc.

Dewey, J. (1939). Theory of valuation. In the *International Encyclopedia of Unified Sciences* 2 (4), 1–67. Chicago: University of Chicago Press.

Driscoll, A., Holland, B. Gelmon, S. and Kerrigan, S. (1996). An assessment model for service-learning: Comprehensive case studies of impact on faculty, students, community and institutions. *Michigan Journal of Community Service Learning* 2, 66–71.

Elshtain, J. B. (1995). *Democracy on trial.* New York: Basic Books, Inc.

Elshtain, J. B. (1997). The decline of democratic faith. In R. Battistoni and W. Hudson, eds., *Experiencing citizenship: Concepts and models for service-*

learning in political science (pp. 91–94). Washington, DC: American Association for Higher Education.

Etzioni, A. (1993). *The spirit of community: Rights, responsibilities, and the communitarian agenda.* New York: Crown Publishers, Inc.

Evans, S. M., and Boyte, H. C. (1986). *Free spaces: The sources of democratic change in America.* New York: Harper and Row, Publishers.

Fitch, A. (1997). Lead analysis in an urban environment: Building a cooperative, community-drive research program in chemistry. In P. Nyden, A. Figert, M. Shibley, and D. Burrows, eds., *Building community: Social science in action* (pp. 74–78). Thousands Oaks, CA: Pine Forge Press.

Fox, M. (1994). *The reinvention of work.* San Francisco: Harper San Francisco.

Freire, P. (1970). *Pedagogy of the oppressed.* New York: The Seabury Press.

Gilderbloom, J., Mullins, R. L., Sims, R. N., Wright, M. T. Jones L. R. (1997). University-community collaboration in low-income housing projects and neighborhood revitalization in Louisville, Kentucky. In P. Nyden, A. Figert, M. Shibley, and D. Burrows, eds., *Building community: Social science in action* (pp. 42–46). Thousands Oaks, CA: Pine Forge Press.

Giles, D. E., and Eyler, J. (1994). The impact of a college community service laboratory on students' personal, social, and cognitive outcomes. *Journal of Adolescence* 17, 327–339.

Giarelli, J. M. (1988). Education and democratic citizenship: Toward new public philosophy. In S. D. Franzosa, ed., *Civic education: Its limits and conditions* (pp. 50–67). Ann Arbor, MI: Prakken Publications, Inc.

Giroux, H. A. (1981). *Ideology culture and the process of schooling.* Philadelphia, PA: Temple University Press.

Giroux, H. A. (1983). *Theory and resistance in education: A pedagogy for the opposition.* South Hadley, MA: Bergin and Garvey Publishers, Inc.

Giroux, H. A. (1988a). *Schooling and the struggle for public life: Critical pedagogy in the modern age.* Minneapolis: University of Minnesota Press.

Giroux, H. A. (1988b). *Teachers as intellectuals: Toward a critical pedagogy of learning.* Westport, CT: Bergin and Garvey Publishers, Inc.

Gorham, C. B. (1992). *National service, citizenship, and political education.* Albany, NY: State University of New York Press.

Greco, N. (1992). Critical literacy and community service: Reading and writing in the world. *English Journal* 81 (5), 83–85.

Gunn, C., and Dayton, H. (1991). *Reclaiming capital: Democratic initiatives and community development.* Ithaca, NY: Cornell University Press.

Gutmann, A. (1987). *Democratic education.* Princeton, NJ: Princeton University Press.

Habermas, J. (1974). *Theory and practice.* J. Viertel, trans. Boston: Beacon Press.

Hannah, S., and Dworkowitz, B. (1992). *Queens tri-school confederation, 1991–1992 evaluation report.* Brooklyn: New York City Board of Education.

Harkavy, I. (1996, August). Service learning as a vehicle for revitalization of education institutions and urban communities. Paper presented to the

Education Directorate Miniconvention on Urban Initiatives: In Partnership with Education. American Psychological Association Annual Meeting, Toronto.

Harkavy, I. (1996). Urban university-community partnerships: Why now and what could (should) be next? *Journal of Public Service and Outreach* 1 (2), 8–14.

Harvey, I. (In press). Postmodernism, feminism, and service learning. In C. D. Lisman and I. Harvey, eds. *Beyond the tower: Philosophy and service learning.* Washington DC: American Association of Higher Education.

Harwood, R. C. (1991). *Citizens and politics: A view from main street America.* Dayton, OH: Kettering Foundation.

Harwood Group. (1993). *College students talk politics.* Dayton, OH: Kettering Foundation.

Hesser, G. (1995). Faculty assessment of student learning: Outcomes attributed to service-learning and evidence of changes in faculty attitudes about experiential education. *Michigan Journal of Community Service Learning* 2, 33–42.

Jacoby, B., and associates. (1996). *Service-learning in higher education: Concepts and practices.* San Francisco: Jossey-Bass Publishers.

Kahne, J. and Westheimer, J. (1996, May). In the service of what? The politics of service learning. *Phi Delta Kappan* 77, 592–599.

Kendrick, J. R. (1996). Outcomes of service-learning in an introduction to sociology course. *Michigan Journal of Community Service Learning* 3, 72–81.

Kobrin, M., Mareth, J., and Smith, M., eds. (1996). *Service matters: A sourcebook for community service in higher education.* Providence, RI: Campus Compact.

Kolb, D. A. (1984). *Experiential learning: Experience as a source of learning and development.* New York: Prentice-Hall.

Krehbiel, L. E., and MacKay, K. (1988) *Volunteer Work by Undergraduates.* Washington, DC: ERIC Clearinghouse on Higher Education.

Kretzmann, J. P., and McKnight, J. L. (1993). *Building communities from the inside out: A path toward finding and mobilizing a community's assets.* Chicago: ACTA Publication.

Kuhn, T. S. (1970). The structure of scientific revolutions. In *International Encyclopedia of Unified Sciences* 2 (3), 1–210. Chicago: University of Chicago Press.

Lappé, F. M. (1989). *Rediscovering America's values.* New York: Ballantine Books.

Lappé, F. M., and Du Bois, P. M. (1994). *The quickening of America: Rebuilding our nation, remaking our lives.* San Francisco: Jossey-Bass Publishers.

Levinson, J. L., and Felberbaum, L. (1993, April). Work experience programs for at-risk adolescents: A comprehensive evaluation of "earn and learn." Paper presented at the American Educational Research Association Annual Meeting, Atlanta.

Lisman, C. D. (1989).Yes, Holden should read these books. *English Journal* 78 (4), 14–18.

Lisman, C. D. (1994) Integrating service with an ethics class. In R. J. Kraft and M. Swadener, eds., *Building community: Service learning in the academic disciplines* (pp. 115–120). Denver, CO: Colorado Campus Compact.

Lisman, C. D. (1996a) *The curricular integration of ethics: Theory and practice.* Westport, CT: Praeger.

Lisman, C. D. (1996b). The engaged campus. In M. H. Parsons and C. D. Lisman, eds. *Promoting community renewal through civic literacy and service learning* (pp. 53–60). San Francisco: Jossey-Bass Publishers.

Lisman, C. D. (1997). Community college service-learning movement: Successes and challenges. *Journal of Public Service and Outreach* 2 (1), 62–69.

Lisman, C. D. (In press). Praxis informed philosophy. In C. D. Lisman and I. Harvey, eds. *Beyond the tower: Philosophy and service learning.* Washington, DC: American Association of Higher Education.

McKenzie, R. H. (1994). *Public politics.* Dubuque, IA: Kendall/Hunt Publishing Company.

McKnight, J. (1995). *The careless society: Community and its counterfeits.* New York: Basic Books.

McKnight, J. (1996, Summer). Redefining community. *The Kettering Review,* 24–30.

Markus, G. B., Howard, J.P.F., and King, D. C. (1993). Integrating community service and classroom instruction enhances learning: Results from an

Marx, K. (1964). *Selected writings in sociology and social philosophy.* T. B. Bottomore, trans. New York: McGraw-Hill.

    experiment. *Educational Evaluation and Policy Analysis* 15 (4), 410–419.

Matthews, D. (1994). *Politics for people: Finding a responsible public voice.* Urbana, IL: University of Illinois Press.

Matthews, D. (1996). Inventing public scholarship. *Higher Education Exchange,* 74–80.

Mattson, K., and Shea, M. (1997, February). The selling of service-learning to the modern university: How much will it cost? *Expanding Boundaries: Building Civic Responsibility Within Higher Education* 2, 12–19.

Mendel-Reyes, M. (1997). Teaching/theorizing/practicing democracy: An activist's perspective on service-learning in political sciences. In R. Battistoni and W. Hudson, eds., *Experiencing citizenship: Concepts and models for service-learning in political science* (pp. 15–34). Washington, DC: American Association for Higher Education.

Miller, J. (1994). Linking traditional service-learning courses: Outcome evaluations utilizing two pedagogical distinct models. *Michigan Journal of Community Service Learning* 1, 29–36.

Moore, T. (1992). *Care of the soul: A guide for cultivating depth and sacredness in everyday life.* New York: HarperCollins Publishers.

Morse, S. W. (1989). Renewing civic capacity: Preparing college students for service and citizenship. *ERIC Higher Education Report* 8, 1–131.

Nelms, B. F., ed. (1991). Community service projects and communication skills—The round table. *English Journal* 80 (6), 89–91.

Nozick, R. (1974). *Anarchy, state, and utopia*. New York: Basic Books, Inc.

Palmer, P. J. (1996). *The company of strangers: Christians and the renewal of America's public life*. New York: Crossroad.

Parsons, M. H., and Lisman, C. D. eds. (1996). *Promoting community renewal through civic literacy and service learning*. San Francisco: Jossey-Bass Publishers.

Postman, N. (1995). *The end of education: Redefining the value of school*. New York: Vintage Books.

Pratte, R. (1988a). *The civic imperative: Examining the need for civic education*. New York: Teachers College Press

Pratte, R. (1988b). The civic purpose of education: Civic literacy. In S. D. Franzosa, ed., *Civic education: Its limits and conditions* (pp. 11–28). Ann Arbor, MI: Prakken Publications, Inc.

Putnam, R. D. (1995a, January). Bowling alone: America's dealing social capital. *Journal of Democracy* 6 (1), 65–68.

Putnam, R. D. (1995b). Tuning in, tuning out: The strange disappearance of social capital in America. The 1995 Ithiel de Sola pool lecture. *Political Science and Politics* 28 (1), 664–683.

Putnam, R. D. (1993). *Making democracy work: Civic traditions in modern Italy*. Princeton, NJ: Princeton University Press.

Rawls, J. (1971). *The theory of justice*. Cambridge, MA: Harvard University Press.

Rifkin, J. (1995). *The end of work: The decline of the global labor force and the dawn of the post-market era*. New York: G. P. Putnam's Sons.

Rimmerman, C. A. (1997a). *The new citizenship: Unconventional politics, activism, and service*. Boulder CO: Westview Press.

Rimmerman, C. A. (1997b). Teaching American politics through service: Reflections on a pedagogical strategy. In G. Reeher and J. Cammarano, eds., *Education for citizenship: Ideas and innovations in political learning* (pp. 17–30). Boulder, CO: Rowman and Littlefield Publishers.

Roberts, B. (1997). Corporation for National Report Evaluation release. E-mail correspondence.

Rorty, R. (1989/1997). *Contingency, irony, and solidarity*. Cambridge, UK: Cambridge University Press.

Rorty, R. (1979). *Philosophy and the mirror of nature*. Princeton, NJ: Princeton University Press.

Rosen, J. (1996). Public scholarship. *Higher Education Exchange*, 23–28.

Sandel, M. J. (1982). *Liberalism and the limits of justice*. New York: Cambridge University Press.

Sandel, M. J. (1996). *Democracy's discontent: America in search of a public philosophy*. Cambridge, MA: Harvard University Press.

Sandel, M. J. (1996, March). America's search for a new public philosophy. *The Atlantic Monthly* 277 (3), 57–88.

Selznick, P. (1992). *The moral commonwealth: Social theory and the promise of community*. Berkeley: University of California Press.

Shor, I. (1986). *School and society in the conservative restoration, 1969–1984.* Boston: Routledge and Kegan Paul.

Sigmon, R. L., and colleagues, eds. (1996). *Journey to service-learning: Experiences from independent liberal arts colleges and universities.* Washington, DC: Council of Independent Colleges.

Smith, P. (1990). *Killing the spirit: Higher education in America.* New York: Penguin Books.

Smith, J. L., and Reichtell, B. (1997). University-community collaboration in low-income housing projects and neighborhood revitalization in Louisville, Kentucky. In P. Nyden, A. Figert, M. Shibley, and D. Burrows, eds., *Building community: Social science in action* (pp. 58–64). Thousands Oaks, CA: Pine Forge Press.

Solomon, R. C. (1983). *The passions: The myth and nature of human emotion.* Notre Dame, IN: University of Notre Dame Press.

Stanton, T. K. (1990). Liberal arts, experiential learning and public service: Necessary ingredients for socially responsible undergraduate education. In J. C. Kendall and associates, eds., *Combing service and learning: A resource book for community and public service.* Vol. 1 (pp. 175–189). Raleigh, NC: National Society for Internships and Experiential Education.

Sullivan, W. M. (1982). *Reconstructing public philosophy.* Berkeley: University of California Press.

Sullivan, W. M. (1996). The public intellectual as transgressor? *Higher Education Exchange,* 17–22.

Summary of Penn–West Philadelphia Public Schools Initiatives. (1998). Center for Community Partnerships, Philadelphia, PA.

Taylor, C. (1989). *Sources of the self: The making of the modern identity.* Cambridge, MA: Harvard University Press.

Taylor, C. (1991). *The ethics of authenticity.* Cambridge, MA: Harvard University Press.

Taylor, C. (1992). *Multiculturalism and the politics of recognition.* Princeton, NJ: Princeton University Press.

Taylor, C. (1994). The modern identity. In M. Daly, ed., *Communitarianism: A new public ethics* (pp. 55–70). Belmont: CA. Wadsworth Publishers.

Vaughn, G. (1982). *The community college in America: A short history.* Washington, DC: American Association of Community and Junior Colleges.

Wals, A. E., Beringer, A., and Stapp, W. B. (1990). Education in action: A community problem-solving program for schools. *Journal of Environmental Education* 21 (4), 13–19.

Wallace, J. (In press). The use of a philosopher: Socrates and Myles Horton. In C. D. Lisman and I. Harvey, eds., *Beyond the tower: Philosophy and service learning.* Washington, DC: American Association of Higher Education.

Wallace, J. (1997). Education for diversity: An approach from philosophy. Unpublished paper.

Wilson, (1997). *When work disappears: The world of the new urban poor.* New York: Vintage Books.

Wood, G. H. (1988). Civic education for participatory democracy. In *Civic education: Its limits and conditions* (pp. 68–98). Ann Arbor, MI: Prakken Publications, Inc.

Wynne, E. A. (1987/1988). The great tradition in education: Transmitting moral values. In F. Schultz, ed., *Annual editions education* (pp. 96–100). Guilford, CT: The Dushkin Publishing Group, Inc.

Wynne, E. A. (1991). Character and academics in the elementary school. In J. S. Benninga, ed., *Moral character and civic education in the elementary school* (pp. 139–155). New York: Teachers College Press.

Wuthnow, R. (1991). *Acts of compassion: Caring for others and helping ourselves.* Princeton, NJ: Princeton University Press.

Yelsma, P. (1994). Combing small group problem solving with service-learning. *Michigan Journal of Community Service Learning* 1 (1), 62–69.

Zlotkowski, E. (1996, January/February). A new voice at the table: Linking service-learning and the academy. *Change* 28 (1), 21–27.

Index

Academic traditionalism, 56–57, 157–158
Action research, 124
Advocacy politics, 92, 113, 125–126
Alinsky, S., 92, 114, 125, 137
AmeriCorps, 25
Apple, M., 72, 82
Association of the New American College, 155–157
Astin, A., 33–34

Bad faith, 78–79
Barber, B., 17, 65, 71, 91, 96, 97, 100, 112
Barr, R. B., and Tagg, J., 27
Bellah, R. N., et al., 69
Berkowitz, Chris, 123
Bok, D., 76–77, 150, 153–155
Bowles, S., and Gintis, H., 80–81, 82, 101
Boyer, E., 156
Boyte, H. C., 14–15, 17, 91, 97, 136
Boyte, H. C., and Farr, J., 98, 110
Boyte, H .C., and Kari, N. N., 25. 101, 104–105, 133, 159

Brandeis University study, 32
Briand, M., 54, 59–60, 106–107, 118–119, 125, 143
Bricker, D. C.,109
Bullard, R. C., 90

Campus and community partnerships, 114–115, 127–128, 159–160
Central Lakes College, 136–139
Citizenship as character education, 53–54
Citizenship transmission view, 54
Civic breakdown, symptoms, 1–3
Civic indifference, 3–4, 61–62, 72, 89, 100
Civic literacy model of service learning, 42, 108–115
    consumerist theory, 70–72
    neoconservative view, 53–55
    social justice view, 85–87
Civic republicanism, 93–94, 150
Civic skills, 105–108
Civil society
    meaning, 13–15
    need, 8

Class reproduction, 80–81
Classic and contemporary
    liberalism, 92–93
Colleges as communities, 156
Commodification of work, 5–6, 78
Commonwealth concept, 15–16, 100
Community as a laboratory, 30
Community College of Aurora, 25,
    115, 139–144
Community college role in civic
    revitalization, 160–162
Community development, 112–113
Community development and service
    learning, strategies, 117–
    126, 141–143, 144–146
Community development model of
    service learning. See Civic
    literacy model of service
    learning
Conns, L., 25
Consumerism, 48, 60–61, 86
Corporation for National Service, 25
Coy, D., 156–157
Critical pedagogy, 78, 83
Critical thinking, 34–35, 66, 107

Daly, M., 49
Democratic self, 104–105
Dewey, J., 27, 63, 69, 98, 108
Driscoll research, 32, 39

Elshtain, J. B., 4
Ethic of service, 23
Etzioni, A., 98
Existentialism, 48
Experiential education and service
    learning, 27–29
Experiential model of service
    learning, critique, 66–68

Fitch, A., 124

Gotham, C. B., 107
Giroux, H., 57, 70–71, 77, 82
Group decision making, value,

    106, 118–119, 125
Gutmann, A., 76–77

Habermas, J., 4, 6, 63
Habit of deconstruction, 107
Harkavy, I., 100, 112, 128, 129–
    131, 158
Harwood Study of Citizens, 89
Hegemony, 78–81, 110
Hesser, G., 39
Hidden curriculum, 79, 83
Highlander Folk School, 106
Horton, M., 106
Hull House, 151
Hypertrophy of freedom, 4–5, 7

Ideological perspective, questioning,
    107–108
Individual liberty, 99
Individualized approaches to prob-
    lems, 3, 7, 19, 69, 94–97.
    See also Privatization
Instrumental reason and pedagogy,
    65–66

Jacoby, B., 32, 42–43
Jefferson, T., 93, 149–150
Justice advocacy, faculty role, 81–
    83, 111
Justice model of service learning,
    42, 84–85

Keynesian economics, 94
Kretzmann, J. P., and McKnight, J.,
    91, 102, 113, 118, 121–
    122

Langseth, M., 138
Lappé, F. M., and Du Bois, P. M.,
    90–91, 102
Leadership, 35–36
Learning circle model of learning,
    134–135
Legitimization crises, 6–7
Liberal communitarianism, 10,

98–100
Liberal neutrality, 42, 154–155

McKnight, J. L., 67, 114
Market economy, value, 49
Marx, K., 5
Materialism, 48. *See also*
        Consumerism
Matthews, D., 79
Mendel-Reyes, M., 76
Moral disengagement, 8
Moral point of view, 104–105
Morrill Act, 150–151
Morse, S. W., 71–72

National Campus Compact, 25
Neoconservativism, 46–47, 53–55,
        94
Neo-Marxism, 56–57
Neo-Marxist theory of justice,
        77–81
New Citizenship, 17, 92
New Westside Economic
        Development Corporation
        (NEWSED), 141–143

Palmer, P., 31, 104
Participatory democracy, 8, 92, 108
Perot, R., 20
Philosophical liberalism, critique,
        95–97
Pickeral, T., 50
Populism, 21
Pratte, R., 96–97, 106
Praxis, 83
Privatization, 3, 8, 14, 16, 47,
        94–95
Procedural liberalism, 109–110
Procedural republicanism, 47–40,
        60, 93–94
Progressive Era, 151
Public intellectuals, 83
Public scholarship, 155–162
Public work, 101, 105
Putnam, R. D., 66

Racism, 14
Rawls, J., 99
Reflection and service learning, 52
Rifkin, J., 2, 5, 46, 50, 66, 96, 101
Rimmerman, C. A., 59, 61, 91, 111–
        112, 114
Robinson, G., 128
Rorty, R., 64–64, 92, 95

Samp, K., 136–138
Sandel, M. J., 69, 93–94, 97–98,
        100
School-to-work, 65–66, 68
Scientism and pedagogy, 62–63,
        65–66
Self-empowerment, 117–118
Service, value, 24–25
Service learning
        definition, 23
        moral development, 26, 30–31,
                35
        value as a pedagogy, 27–31
        value for community, 40–41
        value for educational institution,
                49
        value for faculty, 39–40
        value for students, 32–39
Shaw Middle School, 131–132
Shor, I., 57
Sigmond, R. L., et al., 41
Smith, P., 160–161
Social contract theory, 48–49
Social responsibility of higher
        education
        activist critique, 154–155
        traditionalist critique, 153–154
Social transformation, 76–77, 83
Strong democracy, 16, 19–21, 93–
        94, 97–108
Sullivan, W., 99, 152, 155, 158
Systemic analysis, need, 14, 50,
        111, 123–124

Taylor, C., 4–5, 63, 69, 98–99
Teamwork, 34

Texas Wesleyan College, 90
Turner Middle School, 130–132
Two Plus Four Equals Service on
        Common Ground Grant,
        141

University of Chicago, 151
University of Colorado at Denver,
        141–143
University of Louisville, 79–80
University of Minnesota, 133
    Jane Addams School for
        Democracy, 133–135
    Public Achievement, 135–136
University of Pennsylvania and
        West Philadelphia, 129–
        133

Volunteerism approach to service
        learning, 16, 26, 43, 50–53
    criticism, 52–53
    the faculty role, 50–51

Wallace, J., 106, 133–134
Weak democracy, 17–19, 45–49,
        92–97
West Philadelphia Improvement
        Corps (WEPIC), 129–133
Wilson, W., 146
Wingspread principles for campus
        and community partner-
        ships, 128
Worker cooperatives, 91, 102, 141,
        147
Workplace democracy, 101–102

Yelsma, P., 118

Zero-sum economy, critique, 85

About the Author

C. DAVID LISMAN is Professor of Philosophy at the Community College of Aurora in Colorado. He has served on several national projects with the American Association of Community Colleges and the Campus Compact National Center for Community Colleges and is the author of *The Curricular Integration of Ethics* (Praeger, 1996), *Beyond the Tower: Philosophy in Service Learning* (forthcoming), and co-author of *Promoting Community Renewal Through Civic Literacy and Service Learning* (1996).

ISBN 0-89789-566-5

EAN

9 780897 895668

90000>

HARDCOVER BAR CODE